STAY HUNGRY

SEBASTIAN
MANISCALCO

STAY HUNGRY

STAY HUNGRY

SEBASTIAN MANISCALCO

G

GALLERY BOOKS

New York   London   Toronto   Sydney   New Delhi

G

Gallery Books
An Imprint of Simon & Schuster, Inc.
1230 Avenue of the Americas
New York, NY 10020

First Gallery Books hardcover edition February 2018

GALLERY BOOKS and colophon are registered trademarks of Simon & Schuster, Inc.

For information about special discounts for bulk purchases, please contact Simon & Schuster Special Sales at 1-866-506-1949 or business@simonandschuster.com.

The Simon & Schuster Speakers Bureau can bring authors to your live event. For more information or to book an event, contact the Simon & Schuster Speakers Bureau at 1-866-248-3049 or visit our website at www.simonspeakers.com.

Interior design by Jaime Putorti

Manufactured in the United States of America

10 9 8 7 6 5 4

Library of Congress Cataloging-in-Publication Data is available.

ISBN 978-1-5011-1597-4
ISBN 978-1-5011-1599-8 (ebook)

For Lana and Serafina

CONTENTS

STAY HUNGRY

INTRO

I'M STARVING

When I started working on this book I thought, *Who the hell are you to write a memoir? You're not an economist, president, scientist, or pro wrestler.*

True. I'm none of those things. I don't even know how to speak right. But here I am, typing the words and some of them even have multiple syllables.

I'm a comedian. My claim to authorship is my talent for making observations about people that come out in a funny way. My comedy is based on my own life, how I come from Chicago, that I'm the son of an Italian immigrant father, that I'm married to a woman who is out of my league, and that I'm easily annoyed by people.

If you're a fan (or at the very least can pronounce my last

name, which is exactly how it's spelled, but still nobody can pronounce it: Man-is-cal-co), you probably knew all this about me already. And if you didn't and are just reading this on the toilet at your cousin's house, well, now you do.

Another thing about me: I'm constantly *starving*. My entire day is planned around food. What's for breakfast? Should I scramble a couple eggs like a normal human, or wolf down the dozen my appetite is telling me to do? There are no leftovers with me. The only thing that's possibly left over is a spot on my shirt. My wife, Lana, and I go to every new restaurant in L.A., where we live, and travel to a variety of restaurants all over the world. I know a lot about food and keep current on the food scene, watch all the chef shows (*Top Chef* is my favorite), and seek out phenomenal food. But I hate the word "foodie" as much as if not more than the word "selfie."

I have breakfast, lunch, and dinner, with multiple snacks in between. My wife will say, "Babe, don't ruin your appetite." I don't even know what that means. My appetite is impenetrable. My father and I sit around, talk, eat, and justify the indulgence by reconfirming to each other how good the food is. In one sitting, we have Italian bread, meat, fruit, olives, olive oil, gelato. It just doesn't stop. We push ourselves to the limit, not dissimilar to the Nathan's Famous hot dog eating contest. We just frame it a little more elegantly. Instead of using water to wash down just one more bite than we could swallow otherwise, we use Cabernet.

Tiger Woods's father, Earl, pushed him to become better at golf; my father pushed me to eat tripe. He said, "It's a delicacy!"

I would roll my eyes and say, "Gross. No, it's the lining of a cow's stomach." My grandfather couldn't even speak English, so we communicated through pasta—rigatoni, cavatelli, pappardelle. As you read this book, you'll see how cuisine always finds its way to the heart of my stories, even if they're about something completely different.

Some food rules of mine: I don't eat around my computer. I don't want crumbs wedged between the Control and Escape keys. Some people say, "I don't shit where I eat." Well, I don't eat where I work. A meal for me is a time to chew the fat, to digest the day while filling up on food, recap, stories. I don't do quick bites, drive-thrus, or eat at a stoplight. I need a proper setup. The dinner table is my informal stage where I work out material. There is nothing quick about my meals. The longer the better. We may even sit so long, one meal bleeds into the next.

Food relaxes me. Not eating gives me a nervous, wide-awake energy. The longer I can go without eating a full meal, the more I can get done. So I don't eat if I have things to do, like perform comedy. The day of a show, I have breakfast and a light lunch, but I skip dinner to get that hungry edge. If you've seen my standup or watched one of my Showtime specials, you know that I'm *constantly* moving up there, working up an appetite like a bear just awoken from hibernation. As soon as the set is over, I must beeline into the dressing room, change into a dry shirt, and head to dinner before I can even talk about what went on in my show. Even if it's one in the morning, I don't say, "Nah, I'm just going to go to bed." Some people just grab a drink post-set. I'm ready for a full-blown spread: appetizers, entrées, desserts, and everything in-between.

Problem is, I am also always trying to stay fit. My wife is like my coach, letting me know when I'm allowed to have something or not. A funny game we play: We act like I'm in trouble or sneaking food every time I eat, like she's catching me with my hand in the cookie jar. In my family, you don't open anything without finishing it. My wife will save one cookie, eating it little by little over the course of three weeks. Lana is so tuned in, she knows by my footsteps as I enter the house whether I stopped for lunch, and she can always guess what I had. Some guys come home and take a shower because they're having an affair. I have to wash off the stench of the onions in my burrito.

There is one major aspect of my life where I don't over-indulge, fill up, or even let myself feel satisfied: my career.

My recipe for success is to stay hungry. I never let myself bask in any glory. My father's voice is like a broken record constantly playing in my head, saying, "Don't get too comfortable! Nothing comes easy for the Maniscalcos! Get back to work!"

When I first came to L.A. at twenty-four to become a standup comedian, everything I owned fit in my car. I didn't know anything about making it in comedy or know anyone in that world. All I had was a dream, a hunger for success, and an insatiable work ethic that came from my father. I can't *not* work. It's like a sickness.

I didn't have a choice about staying hungry—metaphorically or even literally—my early years in L.A., working as a "cocktail waitress" at the Four Seasons Windows Lounge and surviving on tips and loose crumbs from the kitchen. I was thrown scraps of hope doing open mic nights and unpaid gigs at bowling alleys and boxing rings, but for the most part, I begged for stage time in exchange for bar snacks (if that).

Even when things did break for me, I didn't let small successes go to my head or fill up my stomach. A taste of success usually turned out to be just that. A sample. A few months after, say, opening for Andrew Dice Clay at the Stardust in Vegas, or touring the heartland on a bus with three other comics and Vince Vaughn, or getting the greenlight to write and star in a network sitcom, I'd find myself right back in that "What's next?" mindset of being between gigs and meals, feeling the hunger.

This insatiable feeling about standup comedy hasn't let up in twenty years, and it probably never will, even now that I'm selling out theaters, touring the world, and writing a memoir. Here's the thing: I'm just as hungry now as I ever was.

In fact, I'm *starving*. I'm going to pause for a sec. My dad just walked in and I'm going to make an antipasti plate. I suggest you do the same!

1

LEFTOVERS

If you want to work in the stock market, you go to New York. If you want to grow corn, you go to Nebraska. And if you want to get into entertainment, you go to Los Angeles. So, as soon as I'd saved what I considered a solid chunk—$10,000—I was going to move out there and become a standup comedian.

Before I headed west, I thought it'd be wise—and considerate—to alert Hollywood that I was on my way. It was a version of calling ahead, like when I was in high school and I called my mom to let her know I'd be late for curfew. She always said, "If you're going to be late just let me know." I would stop whatever I was doing—dancing at the nightclub, having a bialy or clam chowder at the Greek diner—make up an excuse to my friends, and sneak off to a payphone to call

7

her. I was the only one of my friends who had to call home to mommy. They had parents who could give a shit. But my mom was a worrier and still is. "Hey, Mom, we're at Omega, and it looks like we're going to be running a little late tonight. I'll be home by 2 a.m. Don't wait up." She always said "Be careful!" and waited up anyway.

Sending the news of my imminent arrival to L.A. was an extension of that. You call ahead. You tell the relevant people what is going on. It is just polite. And I already had a head shot to use, taken by a professional photographer.

That's a story in and of itself. In college, I heard one of those Barbizon ads on the radio that said, "Do you think you have what it takes to be a model? Come down to the Hilton this Saturday dressed to impress and meet one of our top model scouts from New York City!"

Every Italian kid grows up thinking he's gorgeous because his mother tells him every day. I heard this even when I had an insane mullet in eighth grade. At twenty-one, the mullet was long gone, and I thought, *I could* make some cash on the side as a model. This is my shot. Finally, I'm going to be discovered. I looked at *GQ* magazines for inspiration about what to wear, pulled together a look by combining pieces from my grandfather's and father's wardrobes, and I went to the Hilton. They handed me a questionnaire to fill out. One of the questions was "What celebrity do you most resemble?" I wrote in Antonio

Sabàto, Jr. Every Italian who grew up in the eighties wished he looked like Antonio.

The Barbizon photographer set me up in a variety of outfits and poses that he called "the shots." One was in Hanes tighty-whities in a stairwell, a shot that said, "I'm relaxed, but I gotta run." He draped a sweater over my pecs for a shot that said, "I'm cold, but I'm hot." I was game. I took it seriously. I channeled the raw sex appeal of Antonio, and I nailed it. I wrote a check for $300, money I'd saved working in the cafeteria, scooping potato salad with a hairnet while trying to pick up chicks. (You know the charm you have to generate to land a girl while dunking the ice cream scooper into hot water between serving the macaroni salad and the slaw? More than I had, apparently.)

A few weeks later, I got my head shots in the mail and never heard from Barbizon again—or got any modeling gigs. The only place my head shot photo was featured was in a frame on Mom's living room coffee table. "Stunning!" she said, and she showed it to everyone who came over.

For my Hollywood announcement, I got clever. I made a copy of my head shot, and using a photo editing program on my computer, I made it look like my face was on a movie screen with a bunch of silhouetted audience heads watching me. The caption: "Coming Soon to Los Angeles—*Sebastian!*" I intentionally didn't include my last name, phone number, or email address because I was building a sense of intrigue and mystery, ratcheting up the anticipation. I printed out a hundred copies and sent them to every agent and casting director in Hollywood. I assumed people would be impressed, and I knew my mailing would stand out because it was in a larger-than-regular envelope and the envelope was black, which was unheard of. They would chuckle at my cleverness and flip the head shot over to look for my contact info, since they'd want to call me immediately. Finding no number and no address, they'd think, *This Sebastian character sure knows how to develop dramatic tension!* I imagined them pinning up my picture, waiting with barely contained eagerness for me to send another.

NOW, I'M AWARE that a more typical path for a comedian is to do standup in your town, get your feet wet, develop some chops, and *then* go to either New York or Los Angeles. But with my trademark delusional optimism, I figured, *Why don't I just dive in headfirst?* Since I'd be in Hollywood, I figured I could do a little acting in movies and TV to make money on the side until I became a successful comedian.

I went out for a short visit first. The only person I knew in L.A. was Dean Vivirito, the son of my dentist. When you're from somewhere other than Los Angeles, you will connect with anyone within ten degrees of separation. We used to live in the same city and didn't hang out once, but you move out of town and suddenly I'm asking, "Do you have toothpaste?" Back then, there was no Airbnb. You slept on the couch of someone you knew, or barely knew. These days, you sleep on the couch of a complete stranger. They could have fleas, bedbugs, hepatitis C. God knows what type of diseases are in the cushions of a strange couch that three roommates have been flicking boogers on and farting into after late-night burrito runs. Dean's place was clean, though. His wife was a working actress. Her career gave me a glimmer of hope that it was possible to make things happen out here.

I was respectful of their space and lived out of my bag. I didn't even use their toilet; I went to the 7-Eleven instead, and I only stayed for three days. When I came back, I wasn't going to sleep on anybody's couch long-term. I'd rather have a cheap apartment of my own than impose on anyone else.

Two months later, I returned to L.A. to stay. All of my possessions fit into a single suitcase. I had my clothes, the $10,000 I'd saved up from working at many jobs, and a stack of stamped follow-up head shot mailings. I used the same image as before with a different headline—"Now Playing—*Sebastian*." I included my contact info on the second wave, which would relieve the anxiety of all those agents who'd been dying to get in touch since my previous mailing. I even upped my cell phone minutes in anticipation of being inundated with calls.

Looking back, I know mailing the announcements was naïve, but I didn't know any better. I did what I felt was right.

Since I was putting in so much effort, I assumed that, out of basic human courtesy—something I'm very conscious of—agents would acknowledge my effort, even if just to say, "You got courage, kid. I like your style!"

I started to learn, however, that Los Angeles was not a "basic human courtesy" kind of town. No one called me or acknowledged my mailings at all.

Meanwhile, I started looking for an apartment and found an okay one-bedroom at the St. James Apartments on Hollywood Boulevard and Fuller for $685 a month. The apartment complex had two hundred units, probably filled with other aspiring actors and comedians. I say "probably" because I didn't know any of them. A huge adjustment to living in L.A. was that no one knows their neighbors. Back home, you could pop over to a neighbor's house and borrow a cup of sugar (why are people always out of sugar?). In my apartment complex in L.A., people didn't eat sugar much less borrow it. The place was so seedy, the only white powder they'd have was cocaine. And unless you were their dealer, they weren't opening the door for you.

One exception at the St. James: I popped into the elevator one day and saw Bill Burr, one of my favorite comedians. I couldn't believe he was in there. It turned out, he lived in the building. I was in complete shock, but I tried to play it cool. He invited me to his show at the Laugh Factory, my first exposure to a comedy club in L.A.

A lot of the other residents hung out by the pool, but I

wasn't into it. A public swimming pool? Taking a dip would be like marinating in a stew of two hundred strangers' scabs and broken dreams. The water *looked* okay, but I could think of ten skin conditions it could give me and I hadn't budgeted for penicillin.

My third-floor apartment faced another complex. My first morning, I was standing at the stove, cooking eggs. I casually glanced out my only window, which was over the kitchen sink and faced another building. I could not make this up if I wanted to: A guy in the apartment across the way was naked, locking eyes with me, and fucking his couch.

Welcome to Hollywood!

Instantly, I closed the curtains. An hour later, I dared to peek out. My creepy neighbor was still at it, humping his Jennifer Convertible. A while after that, he was standing full frontal nude in the window. He was *always* there, always naked. I guess he didn't have a job or any hobbies, other than being a furniture lover.

I called the St. James management to ask if I could change units. I explained why. The landlord said, "Oh, that's just Paul. He's harmless." Tell that to the poor couch!

Harmless or not, I still wanted to move. The landlord told me that when another place opened up, he'd let me know, but it might be a while. In the meantime, I kept my curtains closed and stumbled around in the dark, which is a pretty good metaphor for my clueless early months in L.A.

I FIGURED $10,000 would be enough to get me started, but I knew it wouldn't last long, so I went looking for a restaurant job. Instead of just walking in and asking if they needed help, I would sit down, have a meal, and decide beforehand if I liked the environment, the people of course, and the food. Only then would I go up to the manager and say, "I just had lunch here and I really like the place. I'm new to the town. I was wondering if it'd be possible to work here."

Invariably, they said, "We're not hiring."

I'd sulk out, wondering if the $40 I just dropped was ill spent. Whenever I thought about lowering my standards and working at a place I didn't pre-approve, I'd remind myself that I was starting a new life, and that it was not going to begin with a compromise. The plan from the beginning was to get a good job in a nice place for a decent wage to supplement my income while I pursued comedy. I'm sure thousands of people arrive in L.A. each month with the same exact plan, and that was why I couldn't find a job to save my life. All those other would-be actors and comedians beat me to them. It was especially frustrating because I had tons of experience. I'd worked as a banquet waiter throughout college, at the Olive Garden, at a high-end restaurant in the northwest suburb of Chicago called the Living Room. In the past, I'd never had a hard time getting hired. But L.A. was not Chicago. Out here, I was competing for waiter jobs with the next Bradley Cooper from Kansas and the next Jennifer Lawrence from New Jersey. One place asked for my head shot, and I was so proud to leave it—"Absolutely! Here you go! I've got underwear in the stairs and sweater over pecs in the weeds, take your pick." Not only did the casting directors not call me back, neither did the failed actor's manager at Il Fornaio.

At the end of three months, I was down to $3,000. I couldn't ask my parents for help; that would be humiliating. I came up with a scheme to beef up my savings until I landed a job. I would fly to Las Vegas, win money, and keep my dream alive. The logic had some holes in it—really big holes, big enough to drive a tank through—but I was desperate. When you feel like you're spiraling, your mind goes down a dark path and you just grasp at any straw to get out of it. I'd been asking myself a hundred times a day, *What the hell do I do now?* The Vegas idea appeared in my head, and I let my imagination take over. I could see myself at the tables, winning, and I became convinced that my daydreams were just one plane ride away from turning into reality. Part of my brain was screaming, *No, Sebastian!* But the much louder part said, *Just don't hit on seventeen, and you'll be fine.*

I got free flights because, after college, I worked at the United Airlines Employees Credit Union and retained my privileges until the end of the month. I took advantage. I did a quick round-trip in a single day to avoid paying for a hotel room. To get to town, I hopped the free airport shuttle. I didn't eat any meals, just licked clean the bag of peanuts on the airplane. The trip was not a mini vacation. It was work. My sole intention was to rake it in at blackjack and to play this one specific Wheel of Fortune machine at Treasure Island. I'd hit it before when my buddies and I went to Vegas for a Spring Break during college, and I won $1,000. I thought, *I'll just do that again, easy, and pay my rent next month.*

I took the airport shuttle bus directly to my lucky casino and searched for the Wheel of Fortune. I went to the bank of slots where it had been before, but it was gone. Since I'd last been to Treasure Island, the casino had been remodeled, and my lucky machine had been moved. I couldn't find it anywhere, and believe me, I looked. I was able to find two dozen blackjack tables. I sat down and changed my bills into chips, stuck to my rules, played smart—and lost $1,000.

It happened so fast! In less than two hours, my money was gone. I went back to the airport with empty pockets, miserable, discouraged . . . and yet, still hopeful. I decided the bad day was a fluke. My daydreams of repeating my past big win were too vivid, too clear, to be wrong. I believed with my whole heart I was foreseeing the future.

A few weeks later, I returned to Vegas and did *much* better the second time. I lost only $800.

I couldn't even laugh it off with my L.A. friends, because I didn't have any. I could have turned to my parents to console me, but when I called home, I felt compelled to pretend everything was okay. In the back of my head, I was thinking, *I will get out of this. Everything* will *be okay*, so when I told Mom and Dad I was fine, it didn't feel like lying. It put a big lump in my throat, though. If my father had had any idea I'd pissed away in Vegas the money I'd scraped together for years, he would have given me a lecture that only a Sicilian father can pull off—the kind that burns your soul over the telephone.

Keeping things from my parents made me feel even lonelier, which didn't seem possible. I wasn't used to this level of isolation. I came from a very bonded family and a tight group of friends who were like family. Although my father was an immigrant, he was Americanized at the salon where he worked as a beautician. He used his gift of gab to talk to people while doing their hair. A lot of my friends' parents came from the old country, too. They did cement work or jobs where they didn't interact with people that much so they would hang out at our place to watch my dad, listen, and learn.

After a shift at Fuddruckers, where all my friends and I all worked, we would go to my house and play foosball in the basement until 3 a.m., the smell in the air of freshly baked lasagna and *tagliatelle al olio* mixed with Downy dryer sheets and the sound of sneaker laces hitting the inside of the dryer. My family loved having people over, especially my mom. She would bring out food for the guests (the secret Entenmann's stash), and we would sit at the kitchen table and joke around over coffee and cake.

The house itself was one of the newer models on the street, and because it sat on a corner lot, it made a big impression. When my friends saw it for the first time—the manicured lawn, the white brick façade—they'd say, "You live in a mansion!" In my neighborhood, our twenty-one-hundred-square-foot home was different from the others on the block. They were one-story ranch houses with aluminum siding. Ours was two stories with a backyard that resembled Mr. Miyagi's. My father had bonsai trees and other exotic plants that should never have been able to live in Illinois. The only thing missing was Daniel-son doing wax on, wax off.

Inside, the house was immaculate, unless you walked down to the basement, where there was a lot of shit my father couldn't let go of. He never threw anything out, including a dry sauna that he had disassembled from his old salon. Maybe he believes the day will come when someone needs to shed some weight for a wrestling competition. Or maybe he thinks this vintage sauna is appreciating in value? Regardless, it's in a crawl space just in case. Most people inherit a property or family heirlooms when their parents pass away, but my inheritance is going to be slabs of "valuable" cedar wood that have disintegrated over time and are ridden with termites. Basically, my inheritance will be a trash removal bill.

So I went from that environment, a welcoming, warm home with tons of people coming and going, to my one-bedroom in Hollywood with a naked man outside the only window.

Months went by, and I was the only person in and out of my apartment. I had left home before, for college, but campus was only an hour away from my parents' house. I could drive home to do my laundry and get a square of lasagna.

L.A. was a four-and-a-half-hour flight away from everyone I knew and loved.

For companionship, even Paul the Pervert had his sectional. But I was totally on my own.

MORE THAN ANYTHING, I was determined not to limp home to Chicago broke (in more ways than one) and a failure after only a few months. It would have been too embarrassing to bear.

When I was growing up, the number one cardinal sin was embarrassing the family. I'd done it once, in third grade. My friends and I carried a kid over our heads at recess. He didn't enjoy being handled like a bag of potatoes, though, and we were sent to the principal's office. The principal at the time, Mrs. Gifford, a petite, white-haired, beady-eyed ex-nun who could have doubled as a prison warden, looked at me and said, "Sebastian, I never thought I'd see you in here. I'm going to call your parents, and they're going to be *very disappointed in you.*"

That struck terror in me. That queasy feeling of doing something that disappointed or embarrassed my parents became the one thing I never wanted to experience again. From then on, I was always mindful not to disappoint them. I was a good kid, stayed out of trouble. My friends were also good kids from good families. I didn't do drugs or drink too much, even when I was in a fraternity. The idea of my mom telling her friends "Sebastian is an alcoholic!" or "My son's an addict!" was enough to keep me away from that.

Anything that would cast my family in a bad light was undoable, unthinkable. I was so overly conscious of not embarrassing them, I became hyperaware of other people doing embarrassing things that, if I did them, would shame my family. Zeroing in on the bad behavior of others did become like a superpower for me. I didn't judge people; but I exercised judgment. I can't not notice or un-see people's behavior, and that insight turns up in my comedy—hence the special *Aren't You Embarrassed?*

My sister, Jessica, never lost sleep over making a bad impression for our family. She was blasé about spending time with us. After dinner, she'd run upstairs, talk to her friends on the phone, and listen to New Kids on the Block. When I asked her why she didn't bring her friends over and hang out more with Mom and Dad, she'd say, "Ugh, they're so *embarrassing*." She was worried about them embarrassing *her*. If I'd had that attitude, I would have been less anxious. But then I wouldn't have developed finely honed observational skills and the senses of a feline. It's an even trade.

What I'm getting at: My goal has always been to make my

family proud. The thought of Mom on the phone saying "My son moved to Hollywood and tanked in three months!" was enough to get me back out there, résumés in hand.

With about $500 of savings left, I expanded my job search from restaurants to hotels. I thought maybe I could work in room service. I popped into the Sofitel Hotel and asked the person in human resources, "Do you have any positions?"

He said, "We don't, but the Four Seasons in Beverly Hills is always hiring. Go there."

I'd never heard of the Four Seasons brand before and certainly never stayed at a "starred" hotel. The nicest place my family went to was a Marriott. I didn't know to be intimidated by how fancy the Four Seasons was when I went over there and filled out an application for a room service job. There were more interviews at the Four Seasons than to work for the CIA. I went from department to department over the course of three weeks, and the final interview was with Sean Laufel, the director of the food and beverage department. He made me sit outside on the couch for over forty minutes. In my head, I was thinking, *This motherfucker. They've put me through all of this and now they're making me wait?* I was so close to leaving, and if I had, it would have been one of those small decisions that had a domino effect on the direction of my life. Without my job at the Four Seasons, which allowed me the flexibility I needed to also pursue comedy, I might have never achieved what I have today.

At the interview, Sean and I sat on couches facing each other in the hotel lobby. I put it all out there, telling him, "I'm from Chicago. I'm new out here and I really need a job. I have a great work ethic. I'll always be on time and will do whatever needs doing."

Sean was just looking at me, smiling. I wondered if he was even paying attention, and then he said, "Your accent really brings me home. I'm from Chicago, too." I was desperately homesick, and by talking to me, he got a little homesick, too. I guess he liked the idea of hearing more of my accent. "You are not room service material," he said. "I need you to be around people. I'm going to put you in the bar, serving cocktails."

A job offer. *Finally.* I said, "Okay, great."

The Four Seasons lobby bar, the Windows Lounge, turned out to be *the* place to be seen in Beverly Hills or to take an industry meeting. Celebrities were in and out constantly. I'd be one of only two guys working there among a handful of women. I called myself a "cocktail waitress" because at the time, in 1998, working in a cocktail lounge was reserved for women. They gave me a penguin outfit and I didn't give a shit. I was so relieved to have a job (and was only hoping my naked neighbor would sublet his apartment to a female nudist friend). And it was all because of my accent. I got my start in L.A. thanks to my Illinois roots. Thank God for Sean. I don't know what the hell would have happened if I hadn't gotten that job.

And so I began my career as a cocktail server. I was the new guy, eager, with a big smile and wide eyes. If I saw my younger self now, I would turn to my buddy and say, "Wow, that guy is green." But I was just awed by it all. It was as if I'd been dropped into the center of Hollywood, where it was all happening. My first day at work, Sylvester Stallone walked through.

In all my years serving food, I'd never waited on a celebrity before. I'd never been close to anybody famous besides Bozo the Clown. I was on *The Bozo Show* with my neighbor John Papadia. We played Bozo Buckets. I lost, and that was my claim to fame until Stallone. All of a sudden, I was serving Sean Penn at his usual table, number 146 on the patio. Very intense, a great tipper, he always ordered spicy tuna rolls. I probably served him fifty times over the years, but we never chatted. He was nice, but he radiated an intimidating energy that said, "I don't schmooze." Over at table 147, I'd take an order from Nicole Kidman. Talk about stunning. She had an A-list glow about her. Then I'd deliver a fruit plate to Shaquille O'Neal. Shaq was a Sunday night regular, and I felt like I was serving a giant. I would give him a dessert spoon with his cappuccino, because you can't give a man like that a tiny coffee spoon. It'd be like a Barbie utensil for him. He was a great tipper, too, always leaving a $100 bill under the plate.

One night, right before closing, John Travolta came in with another guy and sat at table 113 in my station. They were both wearing workout clothes so I assumed the other guy was Travolta's trainer. I greeted them within three minutes (the bar rule) and put down the nuts caddy (our famous bar snack). Travolta glanced at the menu and ordered a burger, which seemed like an odd choice at midnight after a workout.

I was starstruck by him, I admit. I'd been a huge fan of his growing up, and serving him a burger blew my mind. Most of the customers barely acknowledged me at all, but he was chatting away, just making small talk. At one point, he took a close look at me and said, "You got great legs."

"Oh," I said. "Thanks."

"What do you do?"

"Oh, I'm a comedian."

"No, for your *legs*?"

"Oh, for my legs." I paused. "I run laps around here getting people drinks, and I played soccer in high school."

"Well, they look good."

I didn't mind that we were two men discussing the allure of my bulging legs—by the way, back then, they were solid. I was flattered. It wasn't a life-changing moment, but I was still a cocktail waitress trying to catch a break. It gave me a lift. Never once when watching *Welcome Back, Kotter* did I think that Vinnie Barbarino would compliment my quads one day.

I ADAPTED QUICKLY to the Four Seasons system, and I figured out how to game it. Technically, I was only part-time. Starved for shifts, I made a habit of showing up in my uniform even if I wasn't scheduled, offering to pick up shifts from the other servers. I'd hover by the time clock where people punched in and ask, "Do you want to go home? 'Cause I'll work your shift for you . . ."

No one *wanted* to be there. The other servers were all actors and actresses who would rather work on their tans or "craft" than fetch *pommes frites* and martinis for snobby customers. I noticed the work ethic wasn't as deeply rooted in them as it was in me. If they said, "I wish I could take off, but I need the money," I'd say, "No problem." I'd wait for the 3:30 p.m. person to show up. If they turned down my offer, I'd wait until the 4:30 p.m. person came in. I'd sit there for two hours, hoping someone felt lazy enough to leave. Nine times out of ten, I'd pick up a shift that way.

The more I worked, the bigger my cushion, so if I ever needed to take a day off to, say, perform comedy somewhere, I could. In the meantime, I worked every chance I got. I *begged* for it. I was sort of like the guys who linger in the parking lot at Home Depot, just in a fancier environment.

At the hotel, there was a cafeteria in the basement for staff. Housekeeping, room service, and servers were not allowed to eat the shrimp cocktail and steaks on the restaurant menus, but the hotel did provide meatloaf, mashed potatoes, and pasta to their workers as a side benefit. You were only supposed to eat at the cafeteria when you were working, but on my days off, I'd put on my uniform and go there anyway to

save money. When I was on shift, I'd eat in the cafeteria beforehand, on my break, and afterward. The Four Seasons fed
me three meals a day.

Let's say somebody came into the bar, ordered a spicy tuna
roll, and then got a life-changing call and ran out just as the
food arrived at the table. According to the rules, I was supposed
to take the plate of untouched food back to the kitchen to
throw it in the garbage. But I would eat it. Or, let's say my favorite dessert on the menu—a chocolate pudding cake; devil's
food on the outside, hot molten chocolate on the inside that
oozed out when cut into with a fork—happened to break while
it was being plated. We were supposed to throw that away, too,
but I would scarf it. Who wouldn't?

Was it stealing? Eating the house food was definitely for-
bidden, but I was only eating what would have been trashed
otherwise. By my code of ethics, that didn't seem wrong. Eating pre-garbage was something we servers helped each other
get away with and bonded over. That, and complaining about
rude, vain, cheap tippers was how I made my first crew of
friends in L.A.

Remember that one other male cocktail waiter? His name
is Dan Westerman, a seriously funny guy. Dan was a furniture
mover who decided at thirty-four to be an actor. So he did what
actors in L.A. do—he started waiting tables. I have no idea how
he got or kept the job. He is a great bighearted generous guy,
but a terrible waiter. His section could have one person in it

and he would be running around drenched with beads of sweat over his upper lip. That said, he taught me all the tricks about working at the Four Seasons.

Dan and I were both pursuing our dreams in the entertainment business. We became tight and hung out after our shifts at St. Nick's on Third Street, a dive bar with a jukebox. We'd have a drink or two, bitch about work, and commiserate over our shared experiences. The nature of workplace relationships is that as soon as you get out of the same environment, you have nothing in common, and a lot of those friendships fade. This proved to be true with most, but not all, of the people I met then. (Dan and I are still friends. He came to my wedding a few years ago.) But when you're in the trenches together, you get really close, real fast.

The Four Seasons provided me with dates, as well. Not dates, as in the strangest, most dry, sweet, strange-textured fruit on the planet. I mean women. Sometimes, I'd drop the nuts on the table—I'm talking about the nut dish—for random female customers and we'd start talking. If the vibe was right, I'd ask, "You want to go to dinner?" Cruising at work wasn't my MO, but if a good-looking girl and I seemed to hit it off, I definitely would not shy away from it.

One girl, a regular, came out with me to a nice Italian place. We sat down, and I bought a couple glasses of wine out of my price range. She ordered the veal scallopini, and I got the chicken picante. It was your average first date: "Where you from?" "How many siblings do you have?" "What are your hobbies?" etc.

After I put down my fork, she looked at my plate and asked, "You gonna finish that?"

"Uh, nah, it's a big portion—"

"Oh, cool. Do you mind if I take it home for lunch tomorrow?"

I thought, *What? Is she making a profit on this?*

It was one thing to eat off someone's plate, but this woman wanted to eat out of my doggie bag? I was taken by surprise and stammered, "Oh, yeah, sure. Go ahead."

I would no doubt feel hungry at lunchtime tomorrow, too. Why didn't she think I would want my *own* leftovers? Did she want to order a dish to go so she would have her dinner tomorrow as well?

Like the gentleman I am, I drove her home, the doggie bag on the backseat of my car. I dropped her off, never intending to call her again. Halfway home, my phone rang. It was her. "I left the chicken picante in the car," she said. "Would you mind driving it back to my house?"

Yeah, I'd mind.

The problem with being a waiter and dating a customer: They think you live to serve.

I said, "Oh, sure, I'll be right there."

I continued straight to my house and polished off the picante before hitting the sheets. I am the type of guy who will take leftovers home, and my wife will make sure to tell me, "Don't touch the eggplant parm! I'm having it for lunch." And I'll say, "What eggplant parm? Oh, I ate it at 4 a.m. on the way back from the bathroom. You better get something else for lunch."

On average, for a six-hour shift at the Four Seasons my first year, I made $130 a night, including tips. If I worked four nights, I'd make about $500 a week, or $32,000 a year. Factor in another hundred per week in free food, my job made me feel like I was living the high life.

After six months in L.A., I'd met my modest goal of not going broke and crawling back to Illinois in shame. I had a job, good food, friends, a hangout, a life. And then, out of the blue, my landlord called to say an apartment had opened up on the opposite side of the building, and I could move over there if I still wanted to.

I opened my curtains for a quick peek, and there was Paul, standing in the window with his dick pressed against the glass, waving at me.

I said to the landlord, "I'll take it."

I moved into an identical unit that faced Hollywood Boulevard. A few blocks away on that street: the Hollywood Walk of Fame, Madame Tussaud's, and the cement footprints of legends outside Grauman's Chinese Theatre. At work, I served the stars. On my own block, I could walk in their footsteps. I was right in the middle of it all. Every day, I could touch, taste, smell, and serve drinks to the life I'd dreamed about.

In terms of getting anywhere in comedy, however, I might as well have been living on the moon. I wasn't doing much in entertainment, but L.A. was sure as hell entertaining me.

2

COOKING LESSONS

One question that comes up a lot in comedy is, "Are people born funny?" Is a sense of humor in your DNA, like brown eyes and intelligence?

If so, then everyone in my family was born with it, and so were all my friends. Nothing was valued higher in my crew or family than cracking each other up with a good joke, the ultimate trash talk burn (my friends and I would tear each other to pieces, laughing so hard we cried), a witty observation, or just a stupid face. I remember being really little, smiling and watching as my parents and their friends belly-laughed around our kitchen table. Making my parents laugh was, for me, like scoring the winning rim shot at the buzzer. We all crave our parents' approval, and I got it whenever I said or did something funny. The sparkle in their eyes beamed directly on me.

It sounds corny, but my family was my first audience, the kitchen was my first stage. I felt the most comfortable there, acting out stories, doing impersonations. An impression that always killed at the table was Christopher Lloyd's Reverend Jim Ignatowski from *Taxi*. I would go into "Ohhhkey dokey" in the way he would say it, and it was a sure home run. These were the early stages of my being a performer. When someone got out of their chair to demonstrate a story, (a) it better be funny, and (b) it better be quick. I would share stories about school and my friends. Dad would share stories about his clients and work. My mom would add the witty commentary and always laugh at both of us. My sister didn't participate in those nights until she was older. As we helped ourselves to multiple servings of whatever was for dinner, we would talk into the wee hours of the night like it was Thanksgiving.

When we went over to my grandparents' house, my goal was to make them laugh, too. Problem was, they didn't speak English, and I know, it's a cardinal sin that I never learned Italian. We were too busy correcting my father's English to learn another language. This communication barrier with my grandparents forced me to develop a way to make them laugh through facial expressions and physical movements.

Meanwhile, in elementary school, I turned the dial way down. If at home my volume went to eleven, at school I held it down to a two, max. Class clown? Not me. I flew so far below the radar, I don't think the teachers even knew I was in the classroom. I was the quiet kid in the back, sitting stiffly, taking it all in, observing the world around me. And then when I got home, I'd wrap my observations into stories and jokes, and present them to my parents like gifts.

The first time I called attention to myself in a big way at school was in the fourth grade, when I had to present an oral book report to the whole class. I was a wreck about it. Get up there, in front of everyone, and talk nonstop for five whole minutes? I had my first case of stage fright, which on top of my being an anxious kid in general was frankly terrifying. I would watch everyone else get up there and say, "Abraham Lincoln was the sixteenth president of the You-Ny-Ted States. He wore a tall hat and had a fucked-up beard," or whatever they would say. *We all got up at 6 a.m. to catch the bus in a snowstorm to come to school and this is the performance you're giving?* I looked at everything as a performance, and I could never handle sitting through something boring. You have to give people something worth the price of admission. If I had been casting a show called *Life*, none of them would have gotten the part. They were dying up there.

I couldn't get up there and continue to put the audience to sleep. I had to show them how it was done, or not do it at all. My teacher, Mr. Fitzgerald, said if I didn't do the report, he'd have to call my parents in for a conference to talk about it. My dad would be pissed to have to leave work. Mom would fret. Whenever my parents were brought in for a conference, my mom didn't care so much about my grades. All she would ask was "But is he popular?" She was bullied as a kid, and she hoped her kids would not have to go through what she did.

I hated the idea of stressing her out or, of course, embarrassing her (as in, "My son flunked fourth grade!"). The only thing that scared me more than doing five minutes in front of a tough crowd of fourth graders was upsetting my parents. I wanted to make them proud.

My father was a great music lover, especially R&B. While my friends' parents listened to the Beatles and Elvis Presley, my father blasted Grover Washington, Ramsey Lewis, Lionel Richie, the Four Tops, the Temptations, and Miles Davis. He would pay the bills listening to jazz sax only. My mother danced to Marvin Gaye's "Sexual Healing" while scrubbing dried lasagna off the dishes.

I felt like I lived in a black house with nothing but black music. When my friends got into bands like Mötley Crüe, I would say, "What the hell is *that*?" To me, metal wasn't music. It was noise. On TV, they watched *Tom and Jerry*, while I was obsessed with *Soul Train*. I recorded and studied it every week to learn new moves. I would go to school, and the smartest kid, Eddie Lobenhoffer, brought in an active volcano he made over the weekend. I'd think, *Very impressive, Eddie. But can you do the Running Man?* Eddie would pop his arm up to answer one science and history question after the next. I'd think, *Good for you, kid, but do you have any idea who Don Cornelius is, or his enormous impact on society?*

The legendary *Soul Train* line dance was way more interesting than a science fair project to me. Don Cornelius, the show's host and creator, with his 'fro and soothing voice, gave the black community a place to boogie, and taught this Italian-American eight-year-old how to groove. All of my idols were black: Michael Jackson, New Edition, Bell Biv DeVoe, Boyz II Men, Eddie Murphy, Richard Pryor, Michael Jordan. Murphy always seemed animated, free, physical, and real, and I gravitated toward that.

The book I chose for my report was a biography of Stevie Wonder. Why him? He was one of Dad's favorites, and according to the biography, Stevie led an incredible life, giving me plenty of material to draw from. But I wasn't going to tell his story. Every kid did his report that way and they were so boring. I had to make mine entertaining for the class to watch and for me to perform. I'd made my parents and friends laugh doing impressions, and I'd seen Eddie Murphy's Stevie Wonder on *Saturday Night Live*. I decided, with the confidence and balls of a much older kid (like twelve), that I'd do my report *as* Stevie.

I practiced for days in front of the mirror in my room. In the school library, I scrolled through microfiche photos of Stevie. I got my hands on a VHS tape of Eddie Murphy's impression and studied that. I couldn't have been better prepared, but I was still anxious. With sweaty armpits, I waited for my turn to do my report, and when Mr. Fitzgerald called my name, I sprang up. I ran out of the classroom and returned a moment later wearing the dark sunglasses and hat I'd seen Stevie wear on TV. For some reason, my father had bought the perfect pair of sunglasses on Taylor Street, a place that saw white customers about once a year (probably my father). He thought black people were snazzy dressers and he always wanted to have clothes that nobody else had. He didn't buy the hat, or glasses, specifically for my report, but some things are just meant to be.

(Quick story about me wearing Dad's Taylor Street finds: One night in high school, I went out to meet my friends in my father's red leather lace-up shoes. If you came out in new shoes or a new shirt or hairstyle, anything different, my friends would rip you to shreds. That night, I remember getting "Circus in town?" and "Are you one of the Super Mario Bros.?" While I was trying to pick up a girl, they started humming the Super Mario Bros. theme song. The unspoken rule was and still is: You have to be able to dish it out and take it. If you showed any sign of weakness, it would be an invitation for them to rip on you even more.)

In my Stevie Wonder costume, I made my big entrance, stage left, my heart jackrabbiting in my chest. As I crossed to front and center of the room, my head aimed up at the ceiling, my neck swiveling, a Stevie grin pasted on my face, I could feel the entire class wake up and then they started clapping. I waited for the sudden (and surprising) applause to die down. Instead of a dry start like "Stevie Wonder was born May 13, 1950," I did an impression of my subject's high voice, and said, "Hi, I'm Stevie Wonder. I was born on May 13, 1950. I must've looked like a girl because when I was born, my mother said . . . [singing] *Isn't she lovely? Isn't she won-der-ful? Isn't she precious? Less than one minute old . . .* "

The class went nuts. I played it up—swaying, pretending to flip my dreadlocks—and kept going with my report. From my opener to my closer, the other kids never once stopped laughing. I got some major howls, some nervous giggles. Kids looked from me to Mr. Fitzgerald, dumbfounded, like, *Can he* do *this? Is this* allowed? *Is he gonna get in trouble?*

Look, fourth graders will, generally speaking, roll on the floor laughing over a fart. But, just maybe, the class laughed because my impression and jokes were premium-quality comedy. This prepubescent audience was stunned. This wasn't *The Jetsons* or *The Flinstones*, this was highly developed *SNL*-type humor. I got my first taste of what it felt like to perform in front of people outside my dinner table circle.

I'd told my second-grade teacher that I wanted to be a standup comedian. Who knew my first set would come just two years later?

After that breakthrough report (got an A; thanks, Mr. Fitz!), I wasn't quite as shy anymore. The kids expected me to be funny now, and I liked the attention. I'd developed this ability at the kitchen table, in ripping sessions with my friends, studying comedians on TV and at the movies, and perfecting my impressions in my bedroom mirror (I had a killer Michael Jackson, too). I developed my sense of humor like the basketball players practiced on the court. But I also had the awareness that if funniness hadn't already been in my blood to begin with, it wouldn't have mattered how much I worked on it.

So to answer the question "Is being funny something you're born with?" my answer would have to be *yes*. I was funny at home before I took my show on the road to school. With the positive response, I let my humor show, and it came out more and more. I worked at it, but I didn't have to try too hard to be funny, I just *was*. Like my parents. Like my friends. I was always around funny people, and that raised the game for all of us. Funny was like food. It was on the table, the source of connection and attention. Funny was how I related to people and, after age nine, to myself.

THE NEXT QUESTION that comes up at lot is, "Can a person learn to be funny?"

If you weren't born with it, but really, *really* want to be funny, can you take a class or something? Can comedy be taught?

Comedy can *absolutely* be taught, just like acting, dancing, and writing. It is being taught all over the place. Type into Google "standup comedy class" plus your zip code, and I bet you can find a class for this weekend within driving distance.

Whether comedy is *successfully* taught, however, is debatable.

Let me back that up. I happen to know for a fact that any person, born funny or unfunny, who takes a course of eight Saturday seminars with a professional comedian at a reputable club, who does the homework and puts in the effort, will be able to pull together a ten-minute standup act. It will not utterly humiliate that person if it's performed in front of a live audience of his or her best friends and beloved family members. But should that person devote his or her life to comedy?

Talent is a determining factor in all success stories. You cannot be talented at everything. I learned this firsthand when I played basketball in high school. I was on the freshman B team. My position was at the end of the bench. And in case you're wondering, no, I did not sit there the entire season. They put me in when our team was up by thirty points or more, when there was no risk of my inability to bounce the ball with one hand turning the game around.

My game was soccer. My mullet didn't really look the part of a basketball player, anyway. It was more of a "Bon Jovi meets soccer" look. Hey, my dad was a hairstylist. Instead of trying out styles on some creepy mannequin head, I let him try them out on me. The mullet was permed. I was the only guy with this look, and I think it was my secret weapon to running a successful fast break. I exchanged tips with the cheerleaders about how to minimize the frizz, get more volume, and whatnot.

No matter how many drills I did, how bad I wanted it, what hairstyle I was trying out, or how hard I practiced, I would never be the next Michael Jordan. He was born with a gift. So was I, but it wasn't for basketball.

LIVING IN L.A., I realized something. Apart from one disastrous gig in my college years, I hadn't ever stood alone on a stage, in a single tight spotlight, a mic stand in front of me and a brick wall behind me. I needed experience, and the only place I imagined getting it was at the Comedy Store on the Sunset Strip.

The Comedy Store was the very place almost every major comedian got started or cut his or her teeth. It still is the place for that. Andrew Dice Clay, Sam Kinison, Roseanne Barr, David Letterman—I wanted my name on that list, but how? You don't just walk in there and introduce yourself to Mitzi Shore, the legendary proprietor who has spotted and nurtured comedic genius for nearly fifty years. She had no idea who the hell I was (despite the fact that she *had* been sent my two head shot mailings . . .). She had total control over the lineups—who got to perform at the club, and when. If you didn't get Mitzi's stamp of approval, you would never step one foot onto any stage of hers.

I'd already sussed out that up-and-comers needed an introduction to Mitzi by someone she knew and trusted. But how was I going to arrange that? I didn't know anyone or anything in or about the comedy world in L.A. *No one. Nothing.* According to what I'd heard, it could take years of showcases and open mics at lesser clubs, tons of networking and schmoozing, before you could finagle an introduction to Mitzi. Even then, she might reject you flat out, or give you a five-minute set on a Tuesday at 7 p.m. when not a soul was there.

After six months in L.A., I was settled in at my job at the Four Seasons and had a stable living situation. So I could finally exhale, relax a bit, and turn my attention to the reason I moved West in the first place: doing comedy, ideally at the Comedy Store. There had to be a way to speed up the approval process. I thought I'd found it when I learned that Sandi Shore, daughter of Mitzi and sister of Pauly, taught a class every weekend in the Belly Room at the Comedy Store. The Belly Room was the smallest of the club's three stages (the other two were the classic standup space the Original Room and a Vegas-style showroom for headliners called the Main Room). The Belly Room was smaller, darker, initially created in the seventies by Mitzi as a female-comedians-only stage (Sandra Bernhard got her start there). In the late nineties when I arrived on the scene, it was open to all-gender performances at night. On Sundays, it doubled as a classroom.

The course was called Sandi Shore's Sandbox. In general, I'm disgusted by sand and was turned off by the name. Sand is awkward to walk on, and gets in between your toes, up your ass crack, and into other places you need a Q-tip to clean. And the price gave me pause. It cost $400 for eight classes, a workbook, and videotapes of all your performances. I'd have to work four extra shifts at the Four Seasons to cover it, but the expense would be an investment. If I did well in the class, maybe Sandi would introduce me to her mother, and I'd get a shortcut to the Original Room.

First day of the class, me and about twenty other people sat at the two- and four-top tables in front of the stage. Sandi, an attractive brunette, walked onto the stage, looked out over the class, and said, "I want to start by saying that my mom and I aren't getting along right now. So if you took this class thinking that I would introduce you to her and you'd have an 'in' at the Comedy Store, you were wrong."

I thought, *There goes four shifts.*

I decided to continue the course with earnest intention, to give it my best shot, and hopefully learn something. Since I knew nothing about building a ten-minute act from start to finish, my skill set could only grow.

From what I understand now, having met many professional comedians, taking a course is not a typical way to break in. When I tell people about it, they laugh at me and say, "*What?* You took a *class?*"

I sure as hell did, and you know what? It was a supportive environment with a lot of bighearted people who were just trying to get better at making people laugh, too. I was happy to spend my Sundays with them.

Every week, each one of us would get on that stage and perform jokes we'd come up with in the interim, like a mini set, and then we'd have a group discussion about it. Not a critique per se, just a conversation about what worked and what didn't. I would describe the tone as encouraging but honest. Even if a guy bombed week after week, we would find *something* positive to say about his act. I don't know how seriously all the other students were about a career in comedy or whether they would have preferred harsher critiques. For me, it was all about practice and positive feedback. In the real world, doing open mics at bowling alleys, you'd get plenty of criticism and negativity. But in the Sandbox, it was all about building confidence.

At the end of the class, Sandi gave us homework assignments from her workbook called *Secrets to Standup Success.* It was a manual about generating material, inventing a stage persona, and writing premise-segue-punch-line combos, "one-line visuals," and "call backs." In the first chapter, we were to plumb the depths of our personal histories for topics by answering questions like:

"What was the worst experience you ever had with your
   mom?"
"What was the worst experience you ever had with your
   dad?"
"Do you have any phobias?"
"What are your three biggest fears?"
"What was your worst nightmare?"
"What do you feel guilty about?"

I remember thinking, *Is this a comedy class or a therapy session?* I didn't like to think about any of this stuff *at all*, much less talk about it in front of strangers. As I developed my act over the years and figured things out about myself, I would touch on a lot of this same subject matter. But at the time, I wouldn't go near it. I skipped the dark questions and stuck with the softer ones, like "If you could be anything in the world right now, what would you be?" Easy: *A comedian who performs at your mother's club.*

Another exercise was to figure out what "type" of comedian I would be. The choices were:

Sarcastic (like Lewis Black)
Egocentric (Andrew Dice Clay)
Underdog (Rodney Dangerfield)
Victim (Larry David, Garry Shandling)

Shy/Reserved (Ellen DeGeneres, Steven Wright)
Opinionated (Bill Maher)
Observational (George Carlin, Jerry Seinfeld)

I didn't do politics (still don't). You have to know your shit inside and out for that, and I wasn't even close. I was opinionated, and an observer, so I decided to be an opinionated observer. Already breaking new ground and inventing my own type, and it was only week two!

I pored over the assignments and prepared for class. It was the only homework I enjoyed doing, ever. I read things I wrote and would go, "Wow! Where did *that* come from?" I'd get an idea, which would jog a memory, and I'd think, *I can branch off and take that further.* My mind was off and running (or at least jogging) around the block doing these assignments.

The best part was watching my set on video each week. I'd watch the other students' performances once, and then I'd just fast-forward past those, and would study mine over and over again to judge for myself how I did. I wasn't going to get raw, brutal honesty from the other students, so I'd have to be my own harshest critic to figure out what went wrong and right.

I had two measures of success for a new bit:

Laughter = working.
No laughter = not working.

I kept detailed records of every laugh I got on the videos, expanded on the good stuff, and cut everything else mercilessly.

Nowadays, I have a more finely calibrated measure of a set's success, which can seem mysterious to other people. I'm looking for a feeling from the people in the audience, an energy that passes from me to them and from them back to me. That feeling is the true measure of a joke's worth. A laugh is kind of cheap. It's what audiences want to do, what they expect to do. But if I feel an inaudible emotional locking-in, that tells me my set is working. It's almost like music, like a rhythm I can speed up or slow down, and if the audience is right there with me, I can take them anywhere I want. I feel in control—no nerves, no worries, just a synchronized flow. It's the greatest feeling in the world.

Now something not working is a feeling of disconnect. I might be making the audience laugh, people might be doubled over, but as a performer, if I don't feel the energy linking me and the people, I think, *Something's off here.* What goes wrong can be subtle, but the effect is obvious to me, and it sucks. It feels like I'm completely alone up there.

Back in my Sandi's Sandbox days, though, I had no idea about the energy, the flow, interacting on an invisible level with the audience. I was just trying to crack people up—and I was succeeding. As the weeks went by, I started to notice that when I went up to do my set, people were laughing more than when the others did theirs. Sometimes, you don't know how good you are until you're holding yourself up in comparison to other people at your level. Unlike the "just for fun" students, I was dead serious about comedy as a career. I wasn't doing this class for nothing, and I worked a lot harder on my set than most of the others. The effort showed. I started to feel the same "I have it" confidence I'd gotten in fourth grade doing my book report, ripping one another with my friends, and at the kitchen table at home. Something good was happening here.

The last day of the course was our big showcase where we would perform our best material for a room full of family, friends, and a committee of professional comedians that Sandi brought in. I invited some people from the Four Seasons to cheer me on, and I was grateful they came (and would continue to come to open mics and gigs for the next seven years).

I killed. I got the biggest laughs by far, and I mingled in the crowd afterward with serious swag. And then the bubble burst. A comedian friend of Sandi's came up to me after and said, "I was turned off by the anger. It was forced and unnatural. You need to work on finding your authentic voice."

I was open to this constructive criticism. When I went home, I studied the tapes with this new perspective, and realized she was right. I noticed the anger was masking my insecurities and that I needed to dig deeper, find the truth within myself, and be real instead of putting on a façade.

Yeah. Comedy is like therapy after all.

I'd watched myself on those weekly tapes a hundred times,

and I hadn't picked up on what this comedian noticed in two seconds. So much for being my own harshest critic.

A LOT OF comedians say that their sense of humor comes from pain, that standups are generally troubled souls, and they, we, are a breed apart with a different mindset than most people.

I relate to always feeling like I see things about the world that others don't. But I can't say where my skewed perspective came from. Not pain and suffering. My family was solidly middle class. My parents were loving, healthy people. No addictions, no abuse, no depression, no jail time. We all have our ups and downs in life, but I'm generally a stable guy. There are days that I might not be as happy as others, but my comedy has always been inspired by a love of making people laugh. That drive comes straight from all those happy nights around the kitchen table growing up.

When I face painful things, like my grandfather's Alzheimer's or my parents' divorce after thirty-eight years of marriage, I don't talk about it—on stage or off—for a while. I let it settle. My first gut reaction is "I don't think this is funny at all." Then, a year or two down the road, I talk about it more and more, I open up about how I really feel, and the jokes just pop out. Like recently, my newly single seventy-year-old mom told me she's gone on ItalianMeet.com. I said, "Mom, I hope that's spelled M-E-E-T." Suddenly, what was once upsetting is funny again, and then it goes into the act.

Someone once said that comedy is tragedy plus time. I think for me, comedy is agony plus time. I agonized as a kid, but there was no tragedy to speak of. When I started out, I directed my angst outward. I had a "look at this guy" point of view, reacting with disgust and disdain at the bad behavior of others. I did have to deal with a lot of crap at work—rude, offensive, obnoxious customers—but I didn't talk about the Windows Lounge on stage. I thought I'd come off like a whiney waiter, which is not funny to anyone. I didn't realize for years to come that the topics I *didn't* talk about on stage then were the very ones that truly upset and disturbed me.

So what disturbed me the most about the Four Seasons? Nuts. In a golden caddy with three sections. As a rule, I brought a full nut caddy to each table. And then I'd have to replenish it on demand, over and over again. People would come in, order a seltzer or a hot water with lemon, take up a table in my section, and polish off seven trays of the nuts. We were required to refill the olive dish, too. They'd slurp down a trough's worth of black olives, litter the pits like spitballs, drip the juice all over the tablecloth, and ask me to go fetch more. They'd always call it some stupid name, like "Can I have some snackies?" They thought the three snacks were an appetizer, entrée, and dessert. No, they were just something salty to make them thirsty for drinks, not an all-you-can-eat buffet. This nuisance really got under my skin. These people would signal me with hand gestures from across the room, pointing at their nut dish, twirling a finger like "another round" of freebies. I'd say, "Of course," while keeping what I wanted to say in my head: "Sir, not sure if you're aware but there are eight hundred calories per snackie, so you may want to get a larger size of pants or take this pair to the alterations lady because your button is about to snap off."

Sometimes, people asked for the ingredients in the dish. I'd have to smile and say, "Nuts and salt." I can't stand it when I'm having dinner out, and someone at my table asks the waiter to list every ingredient in a dish and where each one came from. I never ask. I just eat. My wife is one of those people (she also orders off menu, which drives me crazy), and if the waiter doesn't know, he's got to go back to the kitchen and find out. It holds up the whole ordering process. When I was at the Four Seasons and someone asked me about the ingredients in the dressing of, say, the heirloom tomato salad, and I didn't know the answer, I'd lean forward slightly and say, "It's not very good." I'd bypass the entire discussion.

Free snacks didn't add to their bill, so my tip would be nothing, but I'd have to run back and forth, refilling the caddy, pouring their hot water, changing their soiled tablecloths, for nothing. And these cheap bastards looked down on me because I was a server. How was I supposed to pay my rent if all these lookie-loos parked themselves at a table to stare at celebs and didn't order anything? Wow, I was angry. Could this be the anger that was rearing its head during my Sandi Showcase?

I was frustrated that I wasn't on the other side of the table, or behind the wheel of a Mercedes-Benz. But this emotion inspired me to be in that position one day. I learned to turn the frustration into motivation or else it would eat me away. You have to find it where you can. I've always loved to discover motivational people. Now I blast Dr. Eric Thomas, the hip-hop preacher, to get my day started out right. Back then I'd watch documentaries about success stories on TV. I knew I'd get where I wanted to go one day, and when I got there, I would not stuff my face with free nuts. And if I did, I'd leave a *generous* tip for the waiter.

A COMMON MISCONCEPTION about standup: It's the same thing as hanging out in a bar with your friends, telling stories, and trash talking each other. The truth is, standup is nothing at all like that. You're not on a barstool with your buddies. You're on a stage in front of a number of strangers. They don't know you, your history, or who you really are—and you don't reveal your true self to them. You are not yourself up there. You're a comedian doing an act.

A lot of comics create shtick, a gimmick, or a persona to do on stage. For me, the Angry Guy was a persona I tried on. I didn't want to be that guy in real life, but it came out on stage anyway. I was uncomfortable with it, and, in turn, it made the audience (or at least that one comedian at my graduation showcase) uncomfortable, too.

For many comedians, it takes years of peeling away their early fake personas to begin to be a real person on stage. It's terrifying to expose yourself like that, which is why it takes a while. But you have to do it in order to really connect with people.

When I roll the Angry Guy tapes now, I can't even watch. They make me cringe. One bit I did then was to arrange for one of my classmates' phones to go off in the middle of my performance and then pretend like he had answered the call and proceeded to have a conversation. Then my joke was to become enraged, rush into the audience, and take it away, yelling and going ballistic. Terrible. It's hard to watch, and so not me. I'm not a rage guy. I'm the guy who spritzes himself with cologne every morning. I'm the guy who irons his underwear. Why was I acting like a baboon on steroids? It's so hard in the beginning of standup to just be as authentic as possible. You're uncomfortable under the lights; everybody is looking at you. You don't know if people are going to take your act the right or wrong way. It wasn't until five or six years ago when I started talking about my family that I noticed a huge change in how the audience responded to me. People liked the raw honesty far more than anger or outrage. I could never have opened up like that in the beginning.

As I said, I *was* angry when I took the course (those fucking almonds), but I am not an Angry Guy. I had to learn to see the distinction. Anger is a loud emotion; my act then was high volume. I was living with quieter emotions, too, like insecurity, doubt, loneliness, frustration, vulnerability—things that, at the time, were way too private to share.

I was only twenty-four years old, and as I've said, *I didn't know jack shit* about anything. I wanted to come off as mysterious, the guy who made people wonder, "Who is he? What isn't he telling us? What's he thinking?" In hindsight, their guess was as good as mine.

I SIGNED UP for another eight-week comedy course. And another. I played in Sandi's Sandbox every weekend for six months. Performing was practice. I was like, "Okay, sign me up for another class, because I have to keep myself writing and stay motivated."

You're probably wondering if my half a year in comedy school translated into any real-world gigs. Did I ever meet Mitzi Shore?

I did meet Mitzi, but that's another story.

And no, I didn't get one single gig as a direct result of the course. Neither did any of my classmates. To my knowledge, no one I took the course with has gone on to be a professional comedian. The one guy I thought was the funniest in the class gave it a good shot, but he quit after a few years. I recently ran into him managing a perfume counter at Barneys Beverly Hills. Come to think of it, I'm due for a new scent. I think I'll go see him.

I had no regrets about the time and money investment, though. Technically, I had been doing standup at the Comedy Store for six months. My marketing mind kicked in. I took the VHS of my final showcase set (not as angry as the first), had a bunch of copies made, and put the Comedy Store logo on the clamshell box it came in. I added a headline: "Sebastian Maniscalco . . . Live at the Comedy Store!" along with my phone number. I now had a nicely packaged tape to send to agents, casting directors, and club owners—and I did.

One of the places I sent it to was the Ice House Comedy Club in Pasadena. I got a letter back, which I've since framed. It said I wasn't ready or seasoned enough to play the venue. If you get a letter like that, you can either get discouraged and quit, or you can stay motivated and believe that one day you'll make it. So I kept it and used it to spur me on and never give up.

Fast-forward seventeen years. In 2015, I performed five shows at the Ice House. The owner—not the letter writer—came up on stage and said, "I've only done this with a few other comedians. This guy is really talented. He's special." Then he gave me a bottle of Dom for selling out all those shows. Nice touch. It was a real moment of validation for me. I knew that I'd come full circle at that performance.

So can comedy be taught?

It took me seventeen years of practice and peeling away the masks to be able to stand center stage and feel as comfortable and relaxed as if I were at the kitchen table with family and friends.

I did *not* learn that in a classroom. So my answer would have to be no, good comedy can't be taught. It takes experience, which can only be endured.

3

TWO DRINK MINIMUM

Ever since I was ten, as we sat down to dinner, my father's first and second questions were "What did you do today? Nothing?"

If I was off that day, I would immediately have to exaggerate mundane activities to make it sound like I'd done a lot.

"Yeah, Dad, I brushed my teeth, top and bottom, put my shoes on the right feet, and had a lunch meeting."

He will never stop working. He'll die standing behind the stylist's chair in his salon, doing a dye job. He'll be folding some woman's hair into tinfoil and he'll just collapse face-first into the bleach bowl.

In our house, it wasn't enough that he work like a man possessed. Everyone else had to, also. I started working young, going door to door in my neighborhood mowing lawns. I shared three lawns with my across-the-street neighbor John Papadia (*The Bozo Show* guy). He was older and would manipulate me into doing more of the work, but we split the money evenly. What I made hardly covered my bills for my medication, which I had to take because I was allergic to grass and ragweed. I was also using my father's lawn mower, which wasn't borrowed. I had to rent it, tune it, replace parts, and pay for gas. One year, I had to replace a blade after mowing a lawn that was so long that I ran over a hornet's nest. There was nothing worse than running down Shag Bark Lane wearing a medical mask while being chased by killer insects.

If my father caught me, say, sitting, he'd tell me to go stain the fence or re-shingle the roof. At age six.

I don't know any other way to live. His work ethic is so deeply ingrained, I feel empty on my rare days off. My wife says, "Relax," but I have to at least skim the pool or change some lightbulbs. I can't help myself.

When I turned fourteen, I was old enough to get a permit to start working an hourly wage at a legit business. I've worked like a mule, one job or another—two or three at a time—ever since.

- I was a busboy at Fuddruckers at fourteen. I was so conscientious, I was promoted to fry guy *at fifteen*. I took pride in making the perfect crispy golden fries.

After that, I was promoted to cashier, the highest honor before becoming a manager.

• For Olen Mills Portrait Studio, I cold-called people to sell them portrait packages, and somehow convinced perfect strangers to give me their credit card information. If they didn't want to do that over the phone, I would send over our delivery guy "John" (me) to their house to pick up a check or cash.

• During college summers, I temped at an insurance agency—filing, making copies. The only difference between this job and solitary confinement was the endless manila folders. I am still wondering if manila is the color or the type of folder!? You know your job is boring when you try to guess the time before looking at the clock, and it's four hours earlier than you thought.

• Holiday breaks, I worked at Honey Baked Ham, glazing hams and turkeys. I wore white coveralls, a hairnet, a hardhat over that, white industrial gloves up to my elbows, and goggles, like I was about to assemble some microchips. In case you don't know (and I hope you don't) how to glaze a ham, you baste it with honey, and then blast it with a blowtorch. The number one job requirement: Don't set yourself on fire. Number two:

Don't burn down the building. I came home every day covered in sweat and smelling like a hog. I would take two showers, scrub myself with industrial soap, and I'd still stink. But I was proud, because the worse the smell, the better. It was proof to my father that I'd put in hard time.

• On Mother's Day, Father's Day, Halloween, any holiday that might inspire a party, my college roommates and I worked as banquet servers at the Hilton Hotel with a bunch of older ladies whose sole purpose was to secure for themselves the best coffeepots (the ones that actually worked, that kept the coffee hot and didn't leak) before the rest of us arrived. To get a good pot, we had to grease the palm of my friend Steve's mother, who worked the shift before us.

• I waited tables in high-end (and low-rent) places. Let me tell you a story about the Olive Garden. Yes, I worked there, and it's a cardinal sin/deep embarrassment for an Italian. When I told my father I was working there, he didn't get it—he was so proud as he told me that he'd also farmed olives as a little boy in Sicily. I had to break it to him that the Olive Garden was not farm-to-table. It was freezer-to-fork. The waiters were required to sing this special birthday song:

From the pasta we make,
To lasagna we bake,
???????? [mystery lyric that no one knows]
We're wishing you a happy birthday!

We hope you will remember,
This fond event forever,
We're wishing you a happy birthday!

It's like family and friends,
At the Olive Garden,
In the true Italiano way
Hey! Hey!

So if you're looking for some fun,
Try hospitaliano,
Have a happy, happy day,
Hey!

There was nothing worse than trying to round up the fellow "Gardeners" to form the house band to sing this song. Problem was, everyone was too busy giving tables their fourth or fifth round of free salad and breadsticks. So I would have to go to the table alone. That's right, I'd have to sing solo a cappella. Not only can I not carry a tune, I didn't know all the words and would mumble and clap loudly over the parts I didn't know. The saving grace was that most of the customers were trying to cover up the fact that it wasn't *really* their birthday and just get to the part where they got the complimentary cake. I often thought the desserts at the restaurant were only for birthdays or apologies for order fuck-ups, as in "Sorry we burned your steak. Here's a complimentary chocolate chip cookie for the inconvenience!"

• And for God's sake, I was Captain Morgan. Fully dressed with a parrot on my shoulder, I made appearances at all sorts of venues. At a biker bar, I'd have to take my regalia in and change in the bathroom. If those guys saw me come in through the front door in costume, my parrot and/or hook would be shoved up my ass in a matter of seconds. Another night, I got booked at the bar where all of my friends were going. I tried to disguise myself and drown out my real voice with my best pirate accent. My friends were relentless and by the end of the night, I had no parrot, no hook, and they had stolen all of my sample shots.

I showed up at every job interview, even for the lowly banquet waiter gig, in a suit and tie. It often looked like I was the one conducting the interview and the guy doing the hiring was trying to get the job. For me, the work ethic extended to appearance. I had to look good as a matter of principle, to be taken seriously.

Why was I so driven? I worked all of these jobs—the good, the bad, and the smelly—to keep my father off my back and to make money, of course. I had rent to pay, even at my father's house. In high school and college, having my own money meant I didn't have to ask my parents for cash to buy a nice bottle of Drakkar Noir cologne, a new pair of Cavaricci pants, or an Italian beef sandwich from my favorite place, Johnnie's Beef on Arlington Heights Road. I may come from a middle-class family, but I've always had a taste for a good meal and a well-tailored jacket. I'd rather drive a 1999 Honda in a Hugo Boss suit than wear tattered jeans and a stained T-shirt in a Mercedes-Benz. Which was a good thing back then, since a Mercedes wasn't about to magically appear in my driveway anytime soon.

DURING COLLEGE AT Northern Illinois University, I won a standup contest, and the prize was opening for a headliner at a venue near campus. Apart from my parents, everyone else in the audience was black. I went up there, introduced myself, paced the stage, and said something that was meant to be funny.

Total silence. Deep space quiet.

I kept going with my largely unformed act—this was pre-

Sandbox, pre–Comedy Store—I didn't even know what a set was. I got nothing, no laughter. Some people coughed, a few groaned audibly as if in pain. I was so grateful because coughs and groans were better than complete silence. I'm the type of sweater where it's not a slight dew on my brow, it's more like Niagara Falls. Once the sweat breaks, the floodgates are open. There is no hiding it. And I still had nine and a half minutes to go. By the end of the set, I looked like the coach of the winning team at the Super Bowl who is drenched in Gatorade.

I was about two minutes in when someone shouted what sounded like the word "sandman." Others in the crowd laughed at that, and then more of them started saying it, too. It evolved into a chant: "Sand*man*, sand*man*, sand*man*."

"Sandman" like I was putting them to sleep?

In a moment of pure wild optimism, I thought they might be chanting "Sebastian."

Somehow, I got to the end of my time and was chased off the stage by a full audience chorus of shouted "Sandmans."

I immediately asked myself, *Who or what the hell is Sandman and why were they screaming his name at me?*

The next day, I went to the library and did some research. I got an answer. As it turns out, a man named Howard "Sandman" Sims, a legendary tap dancer, used to pour sand on the stage at the iconic Apollo Theater in Harlem and tap dance on it, hence the nickname. But the Sandman was also known by another handle: the Executioner. For decades at the Apollo, when a performer bombed, the crowd would scream and boo and shout "Sandman." That was Howard Sims's cue to tap dance on stage, sometimes brandishing a toy pistol, and literally chase the performer into the wings.

Shouting "Sandman" instead of, say, the traditional white redneck tradition "You suck! Get off the frickin' stage!" became a thing for black audiences at the Apollo and elsewhere, including comedy clubs outside Chicago in the nineties.

As I read more about him, I realized what an incredible, resilient performer Sims was (he died at eighty-six in 2003). His first time at the Apollo, he'd entered a dancing contest and was kicked off the stage. Same thing for his second and third times. For ten consecutive times, he was booted. But the eleventh time, he won the contest. And the twelfth. And the thirteenth. Sims won twenty-five times in a row. He won so many times, the Apollo declared him the official all-time champion, and established a four-win limit for all future competitors.

This guy didn't know how to quit.

Once I'd read that incredible story, I felt proud of my Sandmanning. I started to chant "Sandman" in my head whenever I felt panicked on stage, to remind myself to keep on coming back. If I could be like Howard Sims, who never quit, who never gave up, maybe one day, people *would* chant "Sebastian" when I appeared on stage.

Flash forward a bunch of years, and the Sebastian chant has been known to happen. I've been extremely fortunate to have fans that get my sense of humor and relate to it. These people get me. I can just give a look to get my people laughing.

I also really get into doing comedy for people who *don't* get me, and won't necessarily relate to my stories about growing up Italian in Chicago. For a long time, every Tuesday night, I performed in black rooms in L.A. It's not like I was trying to relive my college-era sweat-shower experience. I just appreciated the honesty of the audience. If you sucked, you got *nothing*. No sympathy laughs. But if they would come around and love you, it was gratifying as hell.

My subject matter doesn't change depending on venue or audience. I do the same set in front of a black crowd that I would do in Scottsdale, Arizona. When it comes down to it, wherever you're from, whatever your background, you'll find something familiar in a genuine act, something to sink your teeth into. I thrive on the challenge of taking a room of strangers who haven't seen my specials, and have no idea what my comedy is about, and getting laughs. It's an incredible high when I pull it off.

Otherwise, it's a sweat shower.

I MET A good friend of mine, Brett Paul, on my first day of class at the Comedy Store. I was shocked to learn that he was an executive at Warner Bros. Television, very high up on the totem pole there. Why would a guy with showbiz clout be in the Sandbox with a know-nothing like me? For him, it was just a hobby, just something to do on a Sunday. He was very funny, though, with belly laugh moments on stage, the one guy I really enjoyed watching. We hit it off, and at the end of the course, I thought, *Now we can go out and do standup together.*

I knew a place, Highland Grounds, a club on Highland Avenue in L.A., that had an open mic night that started at 10 p.m. I said to Brett, "Let's do it."

He said, "Can't."

"Come on, man, it'll be fun."

"Sebastian, I got a *job*."

Oh, yeah. He was a hot shit lawyer at a major production company.

"You have to do it at least once," I said, and kept at him until he agreed to go with me. I didn't want to do it by myself! I needed one person in the audience to laugh at my jokes.

Highland Grounds was open mic for *everything*—musicians, comedians, singers, jugglers—not specifically for standup. Brett and I showed up at 10 p.m.—he was already yawning—and waited in the back for an hour and a half, watching a bunch of awful performances. Finally, it was our turn. He went up first and did his act. I looked around and realized I was the only one paying *any* attention. The other people were tuning guitars, practicing plate spinning, warming up harmonicas, waiting for their turn.

I got up and went straight into my act. I stuck to the script, no improv, no catering to the crowd, which equaled no laughs. No one bothered to respond or seemed aware I'd spoken at all. *Did anyone show up to just watch the show?* As soon as I had the thought, I swear to God, I heard someone doing voice warm-ups in the back of the room, "La la la la la la lahhhhh."

To do comedy, you need an audience. Otherwise, you're just making jokes in a dark room. Don't get me wrong, I have been known to crack myself up on occasion. But there's no way to know if what you think is funny is also funny to others unless you put it out there. At Highland Grounds, I was *way* out there, but as far as the audience was concerned, I was invisible.

From his seat in the back, Brett smiled gamely at me. It felt like I was only performing for him.

I thought, *Okay, they're not listening now. But as soon as that guy stops tuning his ukulele, they're all going to pay attention.*

With grit and determination, I dug into my set, really getting into it, acing my premises and setups, nailing my punch lines. If Sandi Shore had been in the audience, she would have been kvelling.

And wouldn't you know it?

Everyone in the place . . . continued to completely ignore me.

Yeah, this is not one of those stories where people suddenly tune in and say, "Whoa! *Who is this guy?* He's really great!"

Nope, I don't have any of those stories for you at Highland

Grounds open mic. You could have been Chris Rock or Andrew Dice Clay, and no one would have looked twice.

On the drive home, Brett said, "I'm never doing that again."

Can't say I blamed him.

Brett reached his limit after just one demoralizing night. I had to ask myself, *How many am I up for?* My father's voice was always in the back of my head: "You don't know what hard work is! Nothing ever comes easy to us Maniscalcos."

I told myself that my hard limit of demoralizing nights was infinity. I would keep on doing this, night after night, three times a night, forever, before I admitted defeat. It wasn't even about winning. For me, the ultimate victory would be to earn a living doing the one thing I love most: standup comedy. I was never doing it for wealth or fame. I just loved comedy and had been raised to equate quitting with death. It wasn't like an "I'll show them!" thing, although I did want to make my parents proud. It was a feeling of never being a person who gave up too soon and let his dream slip away.

Ironically named, Highland Grounds was a low point. But it was also symbolic. I was starting at the bottom and had nowhere to go but up. From that night on, if there was an open mic anywhere in L.A., I'd be in the back of the room, waiting for my turn to stand in front of it. While the other comedians were comparing notes and bragging about how their set killed at a comedy room at Miyagi's (sushi) or Miceli's (Italian) the night before, I would isolate myself from all of them. I'd study the crowd and go over my notes before it was my turn to go on.

I did hundreds of bringer shows, where you had to bring in a certain number of people to get a spot on stage and do your set for free. The way it worked: I would give the promoter a list of six or seven names of people I had coming, and I'd make sure they all checked in at the front door. Even more awkward than being ignored on stage was the weekly task of asking friends, coworkers at the Four Seasons, anyone I met, to come see me perform.

It was a big ask, and I hated doing it. Roping someone into seeing your comedy show isn't like asking them to sign a petition or write a Yelp review. They had to give up a free night; drive across town; pay for gas, parking, a cover charge, and a two drink minimum; and sit through twelve other comedians until I did my act, which, at the time, was kind of painful to watch. My soft sell went something like this: "Hey, Katie. I'm doing standup at Lucky Strike Bowling Alley tonight. If you want to come, let me know."

Katie would say, "What? A bowling alley [boxing ring, veteran hall, strip club]? You can do comedy there?"

"Ya, it's really great," I'd say. "You never know who is going to be there. It's right in Hollywood so there might be someone in the industry there. It's a little hard to hear over the crashing of the bowling pins, but I get a free round of bowling, so we can hit the lanes afterward."

I never pushed it. I never begged or even explained that if I didn't get the requisite number of bodies (with a pulse and cash), I wouldn't get to perform at all. I just told people about the show, and because they liked me or thought I was funny already, a lot of the times they would come. I would only ask the same person twice, though. After that, it gets awkward. Before long, you run out of people to ask.

I convinced the general manager of the Four Seasons, an Englishman, to come one night. I don't think he understood why I was doing standup. "But you work here," he said. He was a hotel guy and just didn't get why I, and 70 percent of his staff, were pursuing other things while waiting tables or parking cars to pay the rent. But he was game and came to a show. I think he was curious how a serious cocktail waitress could possibly tell a joke and make a crowd of people laugh. Years later when my standup career picked up, every time I saw him around the hotel, he asked, in a condescending British voice, "Are you *still* doing comedy?"

And then I imagined asking him, "Do you *still* think I want to serve Lemon Drop Martinis for the rest of my life?"

AFTER TWO YEARS of open mics, playing to sparse crowds and sometimes no crowds, I developed a solid ten to fifteen minutes of material. I knew I had some good stuff because I was making waiters, busboys, and other comedians laugh.

It was time to reach for a better class of venue.

The Comedy Store had an open mic night, too, on Sundays between 7 and 9 p.m., but it wasn't like you could just show up with five friends and go on. There was a system in place. All first-timers were to come to the Store on Sunday afternoon, along with fifty other comedians, to pick a slip of paper literally out of a hat. Most of the slips were blank, but twenty of them had a number on them. If you picked a number, it meant that you would do three minutes at the following Sunday night's open mic. The number itself was the order of when you'd go on. So if you picked the number one, you'd go on first. If you picked twenty, you'd go on last.

I went to that lottery every week and waited outside in the parking lot for five or six hours to put my hand in that hat, and then I got the blank slips for weeks in a row. Back then, there was only two-hour parking by the Store, so I would have to keep running back and forth to my car to put money in the meter. At that time, a parking ticket could set me back weeks. I kept returning every Sunday, regardless. Sooner or later, I told myself, my number was going to come up.

And it did. I got number fifteen, meaning I would be the fifteenth comedian to perform the following Sunday, so I could expect to get on stage around 8:30 p.m. This was good. The later you went on, the more people were in the room, including the "paid regulars." They started showing up at the tail end of open mic hours to have a drink or two and hang out with their friends before they'd do their sets starting at nine. Everyone knew that if you could make a regular laugh, he or she might recommend you to do a showcase for Mitzi Shore. And then, if she really liked you, she'd put you on the paid roster.

I spent the week before my open mic slot polishing my material. Then after what felt like forever, Sunday came around. I went to the Comedy Store, squeezed inside, and waited in the back for the fourteen comedians before me to finish. Finally, I heard the MC Bob Oschack call my name. With my black Liz Claiborne suit and light blue button-down shirt, I marched my cheesy ass onto the stage and did my three minutes.

Shortest three minutes in my life.

I'd built it up so much in my mind, with so much adrenaline and anticipation, and then it was over before my brain processed that it was actually happening. But at least I didn't freeze. I think I did well. People seemed to like it, but I wasn't sure. I got off stage and the next guy went up. I remember walking to the back of the room to catch my breath.

A bear of a guy ambled over to me and indicated with a head wag to step outside. I did and he followed. Once we were outside, he extended his hand and said, "I'm Wheels. I liked what you were doing up there. I'm going to recommend you to Mitzi."

Just like that, Michael "Wheels" Parise, Comedy Store regular and longtime member of the Andrew Dice Clay posse, became my sponsor. He set me up to do a showcase for Mitzi Shore.

Mitzi wasn't at the club too often in those days because she was dealing with some health issues. But she did come in for an hour showcase once a week. So I was one of a small group of aspiring comedians who got on stage and did three minutes for her while she sat in the back of the room.

Seeing her for the first time, I will never forget the presence she had. If her aura could talk, it would say, "Do not speak unless spoken to." Mitzi is the Anna Wintour of comedy.

With her go-ahead, I did the same three minutes I'd done at the open mic. Afterward, she called me over with the wave of her hand. I stood in front of her, ready to thank her for the opportunity and gush like a polite Italian boy. But she didn't give me the chance. Before I could speak, she said, "I want to see you for ten minutes."

It was like a callback. I went back to the next showcase and did my ten-minute set. As I walked off stage, she said, "How long you in town?"

I was surprised by her question and didn't know how to answer. I was afraid if I said I lived here, she'd say, "Pack your suitcase and go back home." If I said I didn't live here, she'd say, "Don't bother moving out here."

I said, "I live in Hollywood."

"Okay." And that was the end of the conversation. I was

dismissed. I walked out of there, thinking, *What the fuck did that mean?*

The next day, to my disbelief, I got a call from the Store's talent coordinator, who informed me that I had been upgraded to "paid regular" status, and could call in for spots at the Comedy Store and earn $15 per fifteen-minute set. A dollar a minute, or $60 per hour, which was a better rate than I was making at the Four Seasons! Of course, you don't get four sets an hour, eight hours a day at the Store. You are lucky to get one set. I wasn't doing it for the money—that would have been insane—but I was starving for stage time, especially *that* stage.

Every night, I called in and said, "I'll take any available slot."

My reasoning was, the more slots I put in for, the more I'd get. But every comedian did that. Mitzi was really generous in the beginning, giving me three, sometimes four spots a week, which was a good amount of time to hone my act.

Once I had my slots at the Store, I would work out how I was going to manipulate my Four Seasons schedule to get there. With my seniority (I'd been there for a few years by then), I was able to race to the Comedy Store and do a fifteen-minute set during my forty-five-minute break. This is how it worked:

1. Exactly one hour before my slot, I would survey my tables and refill everybody's drink, water, and nut caddy.

2. I would use the bar's landline to call the Store and ask if they were on schedule, while pretending like I was taking a phone order. Often, the Store's schedule was off because someone like Eddie Griffin had popped in to do a set. When a famous comedian popped in, he or she went on stage immediately for as long as the comedian liked, throwing the entire night's schedule off. Funny that it's called a "set" when the timing is fluid.

3. If they were on time, I would leave the Four Seasons ten minutes before my start time at the Store.

4. I'd drive over there in eight minutes flat. I was like the Waze app before it existed. At stoplights, I changed out of my waiter uniform into nice slacks. I threw on a show shirt I had picked up on the part of Melrose nobody should go to. That clothing store had to be a front for drugs and laundered money. I was the only asshole purchasing the see-through snakeskin button-downs in the "Attitudes for Men" window display. If the stoplights didn't allow me to change, I would wear my Four Seasons uniform on stage. One time, when I was waiting to go up, someone asked me to get them a Midori Sour. I had even left my nametag on.

5. After the set ended, I'd race back in time to clock in again and not get in trouble with the hotel manager.

I spent as much time in the car going back and forth to the Store as I did on stage. But it was worth it. I made the Comedy Store my home base, and it still is to this day.

I WAS DOING other shows at other clubs, too. The more I worked, the more opportunities I'd find. Just by bouncing around, I started meeting people in the comedy community. Someone might see my act and say, "Hey, I got a show in the back room of a restaurant. You should come by," and I would. Pay, no pay, I didn't care. I could pay for my life with the money I was making at the Windows Lounge. My pay for comedy was stage time, honing my craft, and learning the beats and the ins and outs of standup.

If the show was in the back room of a restaurant, I'd try the food. Not for free. Nothing was handed to me for free, ever. But, as you know, I am perpetually starving, and if I saw a plate of ribs go by, I'd have to place an order for myself—but always after the show. I learned this early on in my career. One time, I had a *zuppa di pesce* before a set. It really throws off your timing if you're trying to tell jokes between burping up clams and garlic!

I never ran or organized a comedy show—not my skill set—but I became known as a guy who would do other people's shows at the drop of a hat. Along with my Comedy Store slots, I was up to ten sets a week. Only a few years in, it seemed like I was on the right path and making headway.

I was also starting to feel happy with what I was doing on stage. My act was evolving away from the Angry Guy and into the Appalled Guy—a subtle but seismic shift. I wasn't pissed off anymore, just incredulous about the bad behavior of others. I cultivated the attitude, started to get the beats, and got more physical, more animated up there.

I came up with three minutes about Ross Dress for Less, which became my signature bit:

Went to Ross Dress for Less. Anyone been to this nightmare? I went in there, and I thought I walked into downtown Beirut. I thought a bomb went off. Everything was on the floor. How are they shopping? What, are they pulling things off the shelf? Saying, "This is not my size," and then throwing it across the room? I heard they had cheap jeans there, and I'm in the store, shopping [mimicking rummaging on the floor], *and I found a pair . . . in housewares.*

If you're lucky enough to become known for a certain bit, and you do it enough times, people will start to associate you with it and recognize you for it. People started coming up to me before I went on at shows, saying, "You're the Ross Dress for Less guy. Could you please do that bit tonight!"

I met comedian Bret Ernst at the Hustler Hollywood sex shop, just doing some casual shopping . . . just kidding (though maybe he was?). Even the Hustler club had a comedy night.

They also had a coffee shop called Hustler Hollywood Cafe, and they made a tasty brew that was sure to get you up! They had a secret ingredient. I think it was heavy cream.

So Bret and I were both doing the Hustler comedy night, and we chatted on the sidewalk outside. I gave him my card, with a photo of me on it, a pager in one hand and a cell phone in the other, with the tagline "You paged me?" and my number. I could have just said, "Sebastian Maniscalco, Comedian," but I had to put my stamp on it.

Bret looked at the card with an expression like "What a dickhead," but in the most endearing way. He could totally relate because he came from similar roots as me. From there, Bret and I became fast friends. He's Italian, from New Jersey, and reminded me of the guys from home. Bret is more outgoing than I am, so he knew a lot of people and started to introduce me around.

I needed the help. I'm not a mover and shaker. I'm quiet. It's not ideal for any performer to have a wall up, but I couldn't change who I am. I think some people in the comedy world saw me as standoffish, but that's not it. I'm like a cat. I prefer to hang back and wait for people to come to me.

WORKING AT THE lounge and running from show to show was taking a toll. The grind was wearing me down. There are only so many hours in the day, and given the choice between doing a shift or a set, I'd always do the set. With fewer hours at the Four Seasons, I earned less and had to dip into my savings. The cushion I'd diligently stuffed away shrank down to nothing, and then I made the fatal mistake of relying on credit cards to get by.

Bo was a guy I met doing extra work on *Days of Our Lives*. He recruited me to sell satellite TV subscriptions out of a mall in South Central L.A. He actually told me that he put the "BO" in "HBO." I entertained the idea because I could work days and thought I could make more money. This mall had been within spitting distance of the Rodney King riots. I realized on my first day that the population at this mall wasn't flush with disposable cash. But I thought, with my determination and showmanship, I'd do well. My take would be $100 per subscription. I figured, on a bad day, I'd make $300.

I stood in that rolling kiosk, using every trick in the book to attract customers. I remember recording Michael Jackson's thirtieth anniversary special and playing that on a loop on the kiosk TV. At one point, there were a hundred people at my kiosk doing the moonwalk and spins onto their tippy toes, but none were reaching into their pockets to spring for a dish. I learned that people who could barely afford their rent did not want to pay up front for a year of TV. Especially when they could come get this type of entertainment at the Baldwin Hills Crenshaw Plaza for free.

From July through September of 2001, and into the holiday season, I sold a grand total of ten subscriptions. My work ethic was so damn strong, I actually went to the mall to open up the kiosk after hearing the news of the planes hitting the Twin Towers. Every store in the mall had their gates pulled down while I was opening up the shutters of my kiosk. I was afraid that if I took the day off, I would get fired and disappoint the Dish franchise manager or, even worse, Bo.

Around that time, I was on the phone with my mother when she asked, "How's it going?" Concern had started to seep into her voice, like she knew what was going on without my having to tell her. I guess telling her I wasn't flying home for Christmas that year kind of gave it away.

"Everything's good," I lied.

"Work's all right?"

"Yeah, work's good."

"How's your money holding out?"

"Well," I said, "money is . . . it's bad, Mom. *I owe ten grand on my credit card.*"

I blurted the awful truth before I could stop myself, and then I started to cry. The floodgates opened up.

I was trying to compose myself and didn't realize she'd passed the phone to my father. He said, "Hey."

I took a deep breath, exhaled slowly, and braced myself for an onslaught of "What's wrong with you?"

"Your mother told me," he said.

"I'm sorry, Dad. I just couldn't—"

"*Sebastian*," he said sharply. "It's all right. You fucked up. It's okay. You're young. You're allowed. Now, listen to me. I don't want you to worry. I'm gonna cover the ten grand."

What? It was the last thing I had expected to hear from him. I blubbered, "You are?"

"Your balance with the credit card company as of now is zero."

"Oh my God. I don't know what to say—"

"Your balance *with me* is ten grand."

"I'll pay you back," I said. "Every dime. I swear."

"You gotta start being smart with money."

"I will be. And, Dad," I said, swallowing back a new rush of tears. "Thank you."

He paused. "You're welcome," he said.

All the people I'd met, all the shows I'd done—in that one conversation, I realized how superficial it all was. My parents' love for me, and mine for them, was the real thing. This one phone call was the most honest, raw, unflinching reveal of myself I'd allowed in years. I was having success on stage and making people laugh, but in that one conversation, I realized that I hadn't even begun to make comedy that was from the heart, that would touch other people and resonate in a deeper place than some bit about competitive shopping.

And now I was fired up to reassess my priorities and reimburse my father. No more restaurant meals, nice clothes, or gimmicky business cards. I put everything I earned toward the

"Salvatore Maniscalco Payback Fund." I wasn't going anywhere or doing anything until I paid him back.

I went back to the Four Seasons and told my manager that I wanted to work as much as possible, any shift he had. It was an uncomfortable echo of what I used to say to Mitzi at the Comedy Store.

"I can give you three shifts a week," he said.

"I'll take it."

I worked Monday, Wednesday, and Friday, and then I showed up Tuesday, Thursday, Saturday, and Sunday in my uniform and pulled the old trick of waiting by the punch clock for all the other cocktail waitresses to come in, so I could convince them to give me their shifts, too. Some weeks, I worked seven nights and eighty hours.

I started sending my father checks, $200 a month, whatever I could afford. I would pay my bills, put aside some cash for living expenses, and then write him a check of the rest. My comedy hours were next to nil.

After six months of this, I called and asked my father, "How much do I owe you?"

"Hold on," he said.

He kept a ledger, down to the penny. "Let's see, you sent $300 last week, bringing your balance down to $7,300. At this pace, in two years we'll be square."

Not for one minute did I ever resent Dad for holding me to every penny. I wouldn't have had it any other way. I didn't want a handout. I believe if you screw up, you can't just skate. There are no free meals, free tickets, or free rides in this life. I'm sure my mother urged him to let me off the hook, but I'm glad he didn't.

My father was a hairstylist, not a banker. Writing me that check for ten large had to hurt him, and that hurt me. I *wanted* to pay my father back, so we'd both hurt less. In the process, our relationship grew tighter, and even more loving than before. He was happy to be there for me in need, and part of how he helped was to teach me to hold myself accountable.

The love and humility of this experience changed me—and my comedy. I was down to only one or two Comedy Store slots per week. Paradoxically, working less expanded my act. Since I wasn't going out, I had time to work on stronger material, and was digging deeper for it, too. I started to notice a change in the laughs I was getting. They came from lower in the belly. Hearing the shift made me more comfortable and more confident.

Time passed. I kept writing those monthly checks to my father and honing my new material. Finally, I got even with Dad, and had climbed to a new level of confidence as a performer.

But it wasn't enough. By now, I'd been in L.A. for five years with not a lot to show for it. I couldn't see how I was going to keep it up for another five years. I'd been lucky enough to get as far as I had, but I knew I could go farther, if only I could catch a break. I was starting to feel impatient for it.

And then, finally, it came.

4

THE PIZZA BAGEL

I met Andrew Dice Clay in the parking lot of the Comedy Store in 2002. I went outside after finishing my set one night and saw Wheels Parise, the guy who recommended me to Mitzi Shore. He was having a conversation with somebody. Taking a closer look, I realized it was Dice, Mister Hickory Dickory Dock. He had sold out Madison Square Garden *twice*, a rock star comedian. I couldn't believe I was hanging out in a parking lot with a guy I listened to and loved growing up.

Dice was a very intimidating presence in all black, fingerless gloves, a big leather jacket, smoking aggressively. The look and demeanor said, "Don't even think about talking to me." I never want to impose myself on anybody. I typically wait until someone talks to me first and invites me in. I sure wasn't about to launch myself at Dice with my hand out like a starstruck fan.

Wheels noticed me, called me over, and made the introduction. Wheels and Dice went way back. He had been Dice's opening act in his heyday in the late eighties, early nineties, and they were still good friends.

Dice drew on his cigarette and tilted his head toward me. "Hey," he said. "Caesare." He pronounced it chez-a-ray.

I smiled and nodded like I knew what he was talking about, but the whole time, I was thinking, *Who the hell is Caesare?*

I'd heard that Dice gave everybody a nickname. Was he bestowing one on me so soon? What did it mean? I looked it up the moment I got home. Caesare is a character in the movie *The Idolmaker*. He's a busboy who the main character, played by Ray Sharkey, turns into a Fabian-like teen idol singer. I *was* a waiter (not that Dice knew that), so it kind of made sense. Or not. Who knows? I was just meeting the guy for the first time. (He would continue to call me Caesare for the next six months.)

So now I was part of the conversation in the parking lot, not that I contributed much. It took about three minutes to understand that when you hang out with Dice, he dominates. When he said he'd seen my act and thought I was funny, I was so stunned, I don't think I could have said anything anyway.

In the upcoming weeks, I saw Dice from time to time at the Comedy Store. He would come do a pop-in set and hang out for a while. One night, he pulled me aside and asked, "What're you doing next weekend?"

It's always funny when someone asks you if you're free before telling you why. I prefer for someone to lead with the activity and then I can let them know if I'm free or not. If it's "You want me to help you move?" then my answer is "No, I'm busy." But if you have something fun and cool to do, then I got nothing going on!

"I don't know," I said to Dice. "Coming here? Working?"

"I'd like you to open up for me at the Stardust Theater in Vegas."

Hmmm, let me think . . . take orders in the lounge or do comedy with Dice on the legendary Las Vegas strip?

So far, the biggest gig I'd ever had was in the Original Room at the Comedy Store. The Stardust Theater held a thousand people, and Dice was asking me to do standup there.

Something else also now made sense. Apparently, Dice had come looking for me at the lounge the night before. I went into work the next day and my coworker told me, "Andrew Dice Clay was here looking for you."

"Really?"

"Yep. Gloves and all. I told him it was your night off."

I said yes to Dice's invite, of course.

My only tiny hesitation was that Dice and I hadn't spent much time together. I didn't know what to expect of him in Vegas, although I could imagine we'd be hitting clubs every night. My only lengthy social interaction with him so far had been after a set at the Comedy Store, when he said to me, "Let's go to Canter's Deli." He's got an Italian look and attitude, but he's actually Jewish, and he likes a nice bowl of matzoh ball soup (who doesn't?). So, at midnight, we went to Canter's Deli. I intended to pick his brain about standup, but I didn't even have to ask. We sat down, ordered the soup, and Dice regaled me with stories for an hour.

Another time, I'd just come home from a closing shift at the Four Seasons and my cell phone rang. It was Dice, calling to shoot the shit at 1:30 a.m. He'd never called me before, and I'd never called him. I had no idea how he got my number. I was still relatively new to Hollywood and to comedy, and a guy I'd watched growing up was calling me in the middle of the night to chat. It was surreal. As I got to know him better, I learned that Dice is a night owl. When the whole world was asleep and he was wide awake, he often reached out to people to keep him company on the phone. I was exhausted, but it didn't matter. I didn't need to talk; with Dice, you just listen.

THE STARDUST, AS you probably know, was a classy, Rat Pack–era casino. When you walked in, you could almost picture Frank and Dean walking through the place in sharkskin suits. By the time I performed there, though, it was kind of run-down—in fact, it would be demolished a few years later—but I didn't care. I never would have thought I'd do a gig at the same place where Scorsese filmed *Casino*, or share a stage with the Dice Man.

The theater itself was a semicircle with hundreds of half-moon-shaped booths with black faux leather upholstery, the kind that hissed when you sat on it, set in rows like stadium seating. It sat a thousand people, but it still felt intimate. A runway off the stage shot right through the middle of the room, so if Dice, or Wayne Newton himself, wanted to go out into the audience, he had that option. At that point in my career, I didn't even consider doing that. I was just happy to be on the actual stage itself.

I was thrilled about getting paid $150 per show, on top of the hotel room and a per diem for food. All I had to do was a fifteen-minute set to warm up Dice's fans. For the same amount of earnings, I would've had to spend five to eight hours on my feet at the Four Seasons, serving beef sliders and dirty martinis.

When Dice and I first arrived at the Stardust, he said, "Check in, then come back out."

Huh? I thought we'd spend the day by the pool, have a couple of drinks. But no. Dice had other plans. "We're going furniture shopping today," he said.

I was not expecting that. A nightclub? A strip bar? I could

see those. But a furniture store? Sure enough, he took me to Kreiss, a high-end furniture showroom, and he made me sit on every couch they had. "What do you think? Lay down. Test it out," he said.

"Dice, every couch is more comfortable than what I got at my fucking apartment. I pulled mine off the street. This one costs seven grand."

Because Dice was performing regularly at the Stardust, he'd purchased a house in Vegas and it was completely empty. So I was brought on to be his opener, and his interior decorator. We looked at carpeting together, bathroom fixtures, rugs, and kitchenware.

Dice had a thing about asking salespeople for discounts. "What's the Pro Deal?" he always asked.

The salespeople were as baffled as I was. "What the fuck is a Pro Deal?" I asked him.

It was the fame markdown. He even put the screws on a kid working at Foot Locker. The kid said there were no discounts, but Dice pushed it. "What do you pay for those shoes? The employee discount," he said.

The sales kid was completely confused. "But you're not an employee."

He looked him in the eye and said, "I'm Dice."

"I don't understand—"

"*I'm Dice.*"

He was goofing on the kid, putting on a comedy show to get a laugh out of me. To him, it was a game to goof and mess with people.

Another time, we went to a grocery store and put hundreds of dollars' worth of snacks and drinks on the conveyor belt. Seeing how big our purchase was, the cashier asked, "Do you have a club card, sir?"

Dice said, "How much?"

"With the club card, you can get a ten percent discount."

"How much?" Totally deadpan.

"It only takes a minute to fill out the—"

"*How much?*"

The cashier didn't get it, the people behind were complaining, and Dice just kept saying the same thing. I remember dying laughing at the chaos he could create with just two words. If anybody else came through with hundreds in groceries, they'd want that 10 percent off and would sign up for the card. But Dice didn't need the discount. He didn't need the Pro Deal on furniture or shoes. But he couldn't resist busting someone's balls and getting a laugh out of whoever he was with. He is a character. I think Dice sees the world as existing for his amusement, and he takes advantage of it.

And I took advantage of being in his orbit. Earning $150 per set was mind-blowing for me at the time. Just to give you an idea of how broke I was when I toured with Dice: The Stardust gave me a per diem of $100 a day for food and beverages. I'd buy a small lunch before the show, and then after the show we'd all go to a dinner, which got comped. So it wasn't easy to spend the full $100. I had to come up with creative ways to maximize the per diem. So, in the morning, I'd call room service and order two eggs, bacon, and a bottle of Jack Daniel's. The booze would get me up to $100. I wasn't going to waste a penny of that stipend. If I was in Vegas for five nights, I would order five bottles of alcohol in total. The room service guy would give me the eye, like, "Damn, you're hardcore." Then I'd pack the vodka, gin, and Jack into my suitcase, bring it back to L.A., and stock the bar in my apartment.

Surprise bonus of the Stardust: One night in Vegas, I met Mr. Warmth, Don Rickles. He did the early show and Dice was the late show. So there I was in his dressing room, talking to the guy I'd watched on Carson when I stayed up past my bedtime in the early eighties. I never missed Rickles on *The Tonight Show*. Every time he was on, it was like lightning in a bottle. His chemistry with Carson was electric. Rickles had the ability to make fun of everyone around him, and still make the person feel like a million bucks. There will never be another like him.

I OPENED FOR Dice for two years (not every single weekend, but very consistently), in Vegas and all over the U.S. Hanging out with him was like getting a doctorate in comedy. We would be doing casinos in the middle of nowhere, say, in Tacoma, Washington, and we had long, midnight discussions in his hotel room or the lobby bar about standup, what to do, what *not* to do. At the time, a lot of the people I'd come up with at the Comedy Store were getting TV shows and movie parts. Dice told me not to worry about what other people were getting.

"Just be patient and wait your turn," he said. "You can't compare your career to your friend's career. Everybody's on his own path. The only thing you have control over is your material and your stage time. The rest will take care of itself. It might come next week. It might come in twenty years. You don't know when it's gonna happen, but it never will if you get distracted by what your friends are doing."

I took that advice to heart. I always felt like I was a step behind, or like everyone in my "class" of comedy was getting A's on the test, and I was squeaking by with a C. (High school all over again.) I couldn't figure it out. I didn't know what I needed to do to get up to that level. And here was a guy who'd been to the top of the mountain, and he was telling me to stop worrying and run my own race. He was running his own race, too. Although Dice wasn't as hot in 2002 as he had been in the late eighties—he drew crowds, but now it was theaters, not stadiums—he was still dreaming big. He wanted to get back to Madison Square Garden. He wanted to do TV and movies. No doubt, he'd get there.

Dice loved to talk, and he could go for hours at a time,

and I soaked it all up. He knew a lot more than I did about the business, and I was grateful just to listen to what he had to say. I've always thought that you never learn a lot when you are speaking. But if you shut up and listen, you can pick up a few things, especially from the people around you who are more successful than you and have been where you want to go.

Sometimes, though, I had to sift through his advice to make sure his suggestions were right for me.

"I got an idea for you, Caesare," he said once.

"Great. What is it?"

"I think you need a prop."

"A prop?"

"Something that hypes up the audience, starts them laughing even before you say a word. Gets you a free laugh."

"Okay."

"You should put a sock down your pants. Just go out there with this magnificent cock. You don't acknowledge it, you don't say a word, and you go right into your Starbucks bit or whatever. The audience will go crazy."

"You don't think it'll be distracting?" I asked.

"Who cares? It's funny."

"It is funny. I'll think about it. Thanks."

I did think about it. I even rolled up a sweat sock and stared at it, wondering, *Should I?* As a young comedian, for a split second, I thought, *Wait, does he even know what he's talking about?!* It was entirely possible he was setting me up, too.

In the end I decided not to do it. My comedy wasn't about bulging cocks. That was Dice's style. Even with his crowd, at his shows, I still had to be me.

MY ARRANGEMENT WITH Dice wasn't a formal thing. If he was going on tour, he'd call me and I'd drop everything and go with him. If I didn't hear from him in a while, I would panic a bit and look up his schedule to see if he had anything coming up. Once you play those big rooms, it's hard to go back to hundred-seat clubs. But it wasn't only that adrenaline rush, and the money (and bottles of Jack), that I craved. When I was on the road with Dice, I was a working comedian. I was supporting myself doing the act. That had been my dream, and with him, I was living it.

During the downtimes, I could have called him up and asked about upcoming gigs, but I felt more comfortable waiting to be asked. When the call came in, I'd instantly do the math: Five shows at $150 each was $750, a fortune for me at the time.

I can't say that every minute with Dice was sunshine and roses, though. I learned some lessons about touring the hard way. His fans were volatile, hardcore. There were some couples, but it was primarily men. There was always a lot of aggression in the room. Before the show started, the crowd would chant, "Dice! Dice! Dice!" Into this ocean of testosterone, I'd come out and do my fifteen minutes about Ross Dress for Less. Our acts were kind of similar in tone, but our material couldn't have been more different. Usually, the crowd would just put up with me. The occasional insult was hurled at me, but nothing too bad.

One night, at the Silver Legacy Casino in Reno, his fans were outright hostile. As soon as I came out, they started screaming, "Dice! Dice! Dice!" at scary volume. The volume of their talking never died down while I was on stage. A bunch of them started shouting at me. It was too loud to make out any specific comments, but I got the idea. It rattled me and that only made it worse. You couldn't show any sign of weakness to his crowd. They'd smell blood in the water like sharks and attack. At that time, I didn't have the ability to go back at them. I just got nervous, cut my set short, and walked off.

I went backstage, and when Dice saw me, he started yelling, too. "What the fuck? Why'd you go off early?" he asked. He was pissed off.

I didn't realize it was such a big deal to cut my act by five minutes. I was thinking, *That's it. I'm done. I'm never getting asked back to this again.*

After the show, we hugged it out and he said, "You cannot bail early. Whatever's happening up there, you have to handle it. You can't let them rattle you. You have to be in control of your own act. I'm counting on you to get the crowd warmed up and to do a certain amount of time. I'm in the back thinking you're going to do fifteen. If you get off after eleven, I have to go out earlier and that fucks me up, too."

Now that I'm a headliner, I understand exactly what he meant. I have a pre-show checklist that I have to run through before I go out there. It's nothing elaborate. I make sure I didn't miss a belt loop. I have my tour manager Georgie shine a flashlight on my teeth to check for pieces of food. I have a Halls to soothe my throat. But I need to go through the ritual or it can mess up my rhythm.

If you're scheduled to do fifteen, you do fifteen. You don't chicken out and walk off because the crowd isn't nice to you. If thousands of rabid fans are screaming "Get off the stage!" it does take epic courage to stand your ground. You are completely alone up there (so alone). You can try to convert them, or just get through it regardless, but you have to stick it out until the bitter end.

That night, I was mad at myself for letting the crowd shake me up. They got to me. It would be years before I mastered the art of dealing with drunks, hecklers, and people who shout during the act. Any rumbling in the audience is a sign that you're losing control. And it can spread, too. If one drunk yells "You suck!" and most of the audience likes the show, they'll drown him out quick. But if you're not connecting from the get-go, and someone starts yelling, the whole crowd can turn on you.

If you have a minute, Google "Bill Burr Philadelphia," and

you'll see an example of a comedian in a hostile environment, and people booing who would not cave. He stood up there, insulting the crowd right back, counting down the minutes until his time was up. He did not buckle, and kept a furious stream of vicious, hilarious insults flowing minute after minute. In the end, he won the crowd over. You can see what a seasoned pro he was up there.

The night I bailed in Reno, I was only five years in and had been doing small rooms, open mics, and bringer shows. I'd never seen a large, hostile crowd like this before. Now I have twenty years of experience under my belt and I can deal with any tense situation. About one in twenty shows, I have to come back at someone. You can't plan what you're going to say beforehand. Every time is different and you have to react in the moment. But here's how I handled certain types of incidents:

Drunk idiots: Recently, a wasted guy was getting heated with someone he thought was in his seat. I looked down at him and said, "Aren't you embarrassed?" The crowd laughed, and the guy sat down and shut up.

Screaming jerkoffs: Nowadays with social media, people feel like they have to participate in everything, and you get someone shouting out random shit. I go, "I'm doing a show up here. You mind?"

Insecure assholes: A certain type of macho guy feels threatened if his date laughs at my jokes, so he tries to say something funny to impress her. I can spot the Neanderthal type easily, and I know how to massage his ego. I say, "Look at this guy. I'm not even gonna bother with this guy. He looks like he could kill me with his right hand." It's a compliment, not that he deserves it, but he'll instantly settle down if you acknowledge his guns.

Opening for Dice exposed me to every conceivable type of rough audience—as individuals and as a seething mass—in large venues. In that way, touring with him was like a two-year boot camp. I needed the training to learn how to handle adversity, how to deal with different groups of people. I developed the skills on stage, but what I learned applied to all aspects of life, off stage as well. Stay calm. Keep doing your best stuff. Meet your commitments, no matter what.

Back then, the growing pains of standup were tough to get through, but worth it. I must have thanked Dice a hundred times for the opportunities and advice. Along with sharing his wisdom, Dice and I became friends during this period. He invited me to his son's bar mitzvah and I went to parties at his house in Vegas. Our friendship was a bit one-sided. I don't know if I gave anything to him, or if I was much more than part of his entourage. He seemed to like the loose connection, and, as I've said, I was just happy to be there.

The end was like a slow fade-out. I wouldn't get a call for three weeks. Then six weeks. Then Dice decided to take a long break, and I never got asked to open for him again. When he picked up comedy touring some time later, he used other acts. I didn't take it personally. I reminded myself of something Dice had told me, about not comparing myself to others or wishing I had what they had. Just focus on the comedy and what happened on stage. Stay hungry and *be patient*. Good things were on the way, I just didn't know what or when.

IT'S BEEN FIFTEEN years since my time with Dice, and now I'm in the position to tap up-and-coming comedians to be my opening acts. Sometimes the venue makes that decision, but usually I get to choose. For a while, I requested tapes from four local comedians, and I would pick one. But for the last few years, I've toured with one main guy: Pat McGann.

In 2010, I had a gig headlining at Zanies Comedy Club on Wells Street in downtown Chicago. The venue set up the feature act and the MC. Pat was the featured act. He likes to tell the story of the day of the show, how he saw me walking down the street, came up to me, and said, "Hey, I'm opening up for you tonight." I was in my own head and apparently looked at him like he was crazy before my brain caught up and I realized who he was. Later, he said, "I didn't want to interrupt you," which reminded me of when I met Dice and didn't want to go up to him or talk at all.

Pat and I got along well at Zanies, and when I returned to Chicago to tape my comedy special *Aren't You Embarrassed?* at the Harris Theater, the venue recommended an opener for me. Pat McGann, again. Clearly the universe was trying to put us together. I liked the way he acted backstage, friendly but giving me a lot of space, which I need to clear my head (like I said, I have my pre-show rituals, and they don't include chatting with people). He mostly stays in his dressing room, doing his own thing. His attitude is like mine. We were there to work.

What sealed it for me was that he sent a thank-you note. I didn't even hire him for the gig, and he thanked me anyway. It reminded me of all the handwritten thank-you notes I had sent coming up—to every person I'd auditioned for or interviewed with for comedy gigs, acting jobs, waiter jobs. My personalized notes didn't seem to get me far, but receiving one from Pat convinced me we were on the same page. He was always appreciative of the work. With me, a little gratitude goes a long way. After another show we did, he gave me two bookends, the lion statues from the Art Institute of Chicago. The thought was nice, but I would have had to ship all seventy-five pounds of them back to L.A. They probably needed a crate. So, in all reality, thanks from my father, Pat, because they are at his house with books on Sicily sandwiched between them.

FYI: All up-and-coming comedians, shelve the arrogance for five minutes and write thank-you notes or send small gifts to the headliners who hire you. It won't work on everyone, but it could turn the tide.

I know what I'm getting with Pat. I know his act. I know he's going to make my audiences laugh. He's not going to swear or tell rough jokes. He doesn't do crowd work, like asking someone in the audience, "Where you from?" As a headliner, you don't want an opener who gives the crowd permission to talk to the comedian. When I come out, if I decide I'm going to interact with them, fine. The opener's job is to go out there, get the crowd warm, and then get off the stage. Pat does exactly what he's supposed to do. He's also intuitive and a good reader of social cues. If someone comes onto the bus or into my dressing room to talk about personal or business matters, Pat knows to politely excuse himself. You don't have to explain things to him. For instance, while on tour, I'm not a guy who likes to hang out after the show. Pat can read when I want to grab a dinner and a glass of wine with him, or when to say "good night" and let us go our separate ways.

Plus, he's a great guy, a family guy with a wife and three kids, with huge potential. I want to help him in any way I can, by producing a special for him and introducing him to club owners and bookers. It goes back to what Dice did for me, exposing me to a different audience, taking me around. He lifted me out of my day job and gave me a little scratch for two years. So now I can pay it forward and give Pat a hand up.

IN 2015, DICE and I reconnected, thanks in part to my wife, Lana. She and I didn't know each other when I was in Dice's world, obviously, but she found him fascinating and she remembered her father loving him growing up. I showed her videos of him and told her some stories. She said, "He sounds awesome. Call him up!"

"It's been years."

"So what?"

Through a mutual friend, I reached out to Dice to congratulate him on his resurgence. Just like he'd talked about in a hotel room in Vegas years ago, he'd made his way back to TV and the movies. He appeared in *Entourage* (which made total sense to me, since he'd always had his own); *Blue Jasmine*, an Oscar-winning movie by Woody Allen; and Martin Scorsese's *Vinyl* series on HBO.

He invited me to go see his sons' band at a bar in L.A. When I was opening for him, his sons were ten and thirteen. Now, they're grown men in their twenties. I went down to see them play and hung out with Dice for a while. We didn't reminisce about the old times or update each other on what we were doing lately in our careers. We just talked about this and that—people we knew, movies, music, comedy. Dice is still a talker, but he's mellowed somewhat.

The vibe was relaxed, chill. It would have been inappropriate to tell him what I'd been thinking: "You were right! I was patient and did what you said. And now I'm doing arenas, too." Instead, I kept quiet, like the first time we met. I enjoyed being back in his orbit for a couple of hours, just two old friends, sitting together, listening to music as if no time had passed at all.

5

HOT DISH

After touring with Dice, I thought everything would open up for me. I did notice a brief uptick in gigs, but nothing that propelled me to the top. In fact, after the blip of attention, I was right back where I was before the Stardust. For another two or three years, my comedy career was stalled. I kept punching in at the Four Seasons, doing spots at the clubs, stagnating. To move up, I needed to impress the right audience. I knew where to find it, but as to how to get there, I was at a loss.

In the early days, Dublin's Irish Pub on Sunset Boulevard was the hottest room in comedy. On any given night, Justin Timberlake, Vince Vaughn, and all of young Hollywood would hang out. Dane Cook was the biggest comedian going and Dublin's was like his comedy home. MySpace was very popular, and he was the first comedian to use social media to promote his act. He became a MySpace sensation (him and Tila Tequila; whatever happened to her?).

If comedy in L.A. was like high school, Dublin's was the popular kid party, and I was the geek who snuck in and stood alone in the corner. I'd heard about it, but I wouldn't have gone by myself to check it out. I was never the popular guy in school or in comedy. In both settings, I always felt like an outsider.

In high school, I didn't play football. I played soccer. The football guys were popular. The soccer team was made up of the kids who weren't big enough for the gridiron or came from immigrant parents who hoped their son would be the next Diego Maradona. When popular kids' houses were TPed on Halloween, my house didn't even get a square. If I was lucky, they would throw the empty cardboard roll on my father's lawn.

In the comedy world, the popular kids were touring the country as headliners while I delivered chicken satay to table 142, my left pec adorned with a plastic nametag.

Bret Ernst brought me with him to Dublin's one night, and I met the guys who ran the room, Ahmed Ahmed and Jay Davis. Nice guys, but they didn't fall all over themselves to give me spots. They had their stable of regulars, and only occasionally gave an opportunity to a newcomer. For a long time, when I hung out there, I was *in* the room, but I wasn't part of it. I wasn't doing spots or mingling or scoping out the VIPs. Most of the Dublin's regulars were invited to Montreal's Just for Laughs

Comedy Festival to do a showcase for up-and-comers called New Faces. A lot of them got network development deals and roles on TV. It was a common path for a lot of now famous comedians to take.

Not me. I was on an island, it seemed, and I was never a New Face. I was a No Face.

Even other guys who weren't popular were doing more than I was to get up on that stage. They would approach the plugged-in guys to ask, "Can I get a spot?" Very often, they could schmooze their way onto the stage, but what did they do when they got there? That was the question. Being an excellent networker didn't necessarily mean you were a great comedian. And vice versa.

My style was to let my act speak for itself. If the guys who ran hot rooms liked what they saw of my act at the Comedy Store, then they'd invite me to perform at their space. Even if I saw room runners at the Store, it was like pulling teeth to go over to them and say, "I want to do your show, man." I would wait to be asked while stewing in frustration.

But Dublin's in 2004 wasn't just any room. If there was ever a moment for me to overcome my discomfort about going up to people and asking for favors, it was then and there. If I couldn't get something going, and soon, I would have to ask myself the tough questions like, *Am I really good enough? Am I wasting my time? Will I ever get away from the Windows Lounge with its nut-munching and bad tippers?* As uncomfortable as I felt about pushing myself on others, I had to start doing it or the invitations I was waiting for might never come.

One night I approached Ahmed and said, "Hey, I would love to do your show." Done. I did it. Ahmed was dealing with two hundred comedians who would "love to do" his show, but he didn't shut me down. I took that as a good sign. He and I started talking, and I became a more visible presence at Dublin's. The next week, he gave me a spot, which was a very nice surprise. When I got up there, my set was funny enough to be asked back. It was like a combo of letting my act speak for itself *and* putting myself on the line.

Even after I got piped in at Dublin's, though, I didn't overstep. Some guys would basically walk off the stage after a set and go right up to Ahmed and ask for another. I would give it a little time, maybe three or four weeks, then I would ask to do it again rather than be one more pest buzzing around his face.

I didn't grow up hearing, "The squeaky wheel gets the grease." I grew up being told, "Grease your own wheel!" For that matter, make your own wheel and grease from scratch. Don't rely on other people to do you any favors. Don't ask for things. Don't be a nuisance. In my mind, working the room and networking would take time and energy away from the comedy, and that would not serve me in the long run. I saved up my courage for when I was on stage.

If I'd had the gift of gab, it's possible I would have gotten a break earlier. But looking back, I think I needed those seven years of warming up before I was ready to get hotter than I was. It was a process, a long one.

So one night, I was at Dublin's, heading for the stairwell where you waited before you went on stage. The space was small, cramped. Maybe three people could fit back there at once. That night, when I walked up the stairs, I saw two other guys were already there. One of them was Vince Vaughn.

Back in 1996 when I was a senior in college, my dad had clipped an article in the *Chicago Sun-Times* about two guys going on a rogue mission to make a movie. My father said, "Look at these guys. They have hardly any money and no permits, and they're shooting on the side of this highway. They went to Las Vegas and almost got arrested. But look at what they did." The two guys were Vince Vaughn and Jon Favreau. The movie was *Swingers*, which was so funny, ballsy, and fresh. Ever since then, I was a huge fan. Flash forward to 2004, in the stairwell at Dublin's, I'm crammed into a tiny crawl space with all six feet, five inches of Vince.

He said, "You're from Chicago, right? I'm from Chicago."

It started to feel like being from Chicago was the key that unlocked nearly every huge opportunity I ever had.

Vince and I started talking about where we grew up (he was from Lake Forest, a well-to-do neighborhood), sports, the Bears, the Bulls, and just bullshitting about Chicago and our teams.

He was at Dublin's often, because he and Ahmed were good

friends going way back. In 1990, they were in *The Fourth Man*, a CBS Schoolbreak Special about teen steroid use (also starring Peter Billingsley from *A Christmas Story*). Vince was a big supporter of Ahmed's standup and hung out at Dublin's when he was in town. I could see how they'd be such close friends. Like Vince, Ahmed made things happen. He was very entrepreneurial, starting comedy rooms and later organizing group tours. I'd heard some whispers that Vince wanted to bring a comedy show to places in the United States that wouldn't ordinarily be exposed to this type of entertainment. The concept was "thirty cities, thirty shows, thirty nights on a bus." Some sketch, some celebrity guests, but the anchor of the show would be four standups.

Imagine my shock when, soon after my encounter with Vince in the stairwell, Ahmed told me, "Vince wants you to do the Wild West Comedy Show." Now I don't believe that my five-minute conversation with Vince got me on the tour. I think Ahmed had a lot to do with it, for which I'm eternally grateful. Vince probably asked him to recommend some people, and I wouldn't have made the final cut if Vince didn't think I was funny. Along with me and Ahmed, the other comedians were Bret Ernst, whom I knew well from the Hustler comedy room, and John Caparulo, a Comedy Store regular I'd seen around but never gone out with socially.

To put in context how monumental this was: The tour was in 2005. In the previous two years, Vince had starred in

Old School, *Dodgeball*, *Anchorman*, and *Wedding Crashers*. *The Break-Up*, his movie with then girlfriend Jennifer Aniston, was coming out. He was on top of the world, one of the hottest names in Hollywood. He had one month off between movie shoots, and during that time, he wanted to do the Wild West tour.

The logistics of it boggled the mind. We were booked to perform a show every night for thirty nights in a row at a fifteen-hundred-plus-seat venue, in sixteen states, covering six thousand miles of the heartland. Vince didn't pull it together himself. He had a team of four or five people handling all that, including his assistant, Sandra Smith, producer Peter Billingsley and his sister Victoria, and publicist John Pisani. On top of all that, a camera crew would follow us around to make a documentary about the tour that would be released in theaters later on.

The whole thing came together really quickly. One month after I got the call from Ahmed, we hit the road.

Our first show was at the Fonda Theatre in L.A. Big Hollywood types were in the audience, including director Taylor Hackford and Jon Favreau. Favreau, who'd become a major director himself, was opening the show by doing a Q&A on stage with Vince. I remember thinking, *Man, if I do well here in front of these people and this crowd, hopefully, some doors will open for me.*

I had a manager, and I invited him to come early to the show because the lobby would be prime hunting ground for him to talk me up and make some contacts. I had to go looking for him that night and found him outside the theater, in the alley. He was drinking a beer out of a brown paper bag like a homeless person with another guy from the management company.

I said, "What are you doing back here?"

He said, "The drinks out in the lobby are expensive so we went across the street to the liquor store."

I wanted to say, "Get your ass back inside and mingle." The whole point of them being there was to get me some buzz. Their job was to schmooze and wangle opportunities for their clients, and these clowns were in the alley knocking down forties.

Needless to say, I changed management as soon as possible.

My sister and her then boyfriend, now husband, came to the show, and I took them on a tour of the bus after. Vince had a "room" in the back, but the rest of us were in bunks that were the size of a coffin. Each bunk had a TV that flipped down, so you could watch in bed, but if you rolled on your side, your shoulder would hit the bunk above you. The close quarters never bothered me. I would have been happy in a van, sleeping on the floor. When I stepped on that tour bus, I thought, *Fuck, this is it. I made it.* Being on the road sure beat delivering a hundred Cosmos at the hotel. For me, the bus might as well have been the presidential suite at the Four Seasons.

The "living room" area had a place to eat, a TV, and gaming consoles. Video games were a big thing on the tour. Vince was extremely good at Madden, the football game. He was smoking at the time, and would light up on the bus. I have a bad reaction to cigarette smoke. Once, I was sitting next to Vince playing a game at 4 a.m. and his cigarette smoke was really bothering me.

I couldn't take it, so I went up in the front with the bus driver for a while. There was a little curtain that separated the driver's area from the rest of the bus, and Vince popped his head through and asked, "Where'd you go? What's wrong?"

"The smoke is killing me," I said.

"I would have moved the cigarette into my other hand, if you'd asked."

Five guys living on top of each other, of course a few of us got sick with the flu. Someone told me to take a Z-pak, which I'd never done before. I grew up in a family where you do not take drugs unless they are prescribed to you. I have this fear of doing it, dying, and people weeping at my funeral, beating their chests, saying, "How could he have taken a Z-pak without a prescription? Why?"

The guys thought that was hilarious, and shamed me into taking the pills. I felt much better, thanks for asking.

Vince was the ringleader with a quick wit. He was another big talker. He didn't go off on endless monologues like Dice, though. Vince held court; he MCed on the bus and on the stage. I think he had a secret yearning to do standup, but he stuck with opening the show with sketches featuring special guests like Favreau, Justin Long, and *Wedding Crashers* co-star Keir O'Donnell. Vince is six-foot-five, handsome, and a *presence*. You couldn't not look at him. Everywhere he went, he drew people's attention, and then, when recognition sank in, they went into hysterics. "Holy shit, is that *Vince Vaughn*?" they'd ask each other. In Nowhere, Oklahoma, at a rest stop in the middle of the night, people mobbed him. It was like hanging out with Tom Cruise. He had to enter venues through the kitchen or there'd be mayhem.

It was so exciting to be in public with him, I remember feeling disappointed when he decided to stay on the bus after a show instead of going to bars and clubs with us. But he was with Jennifer Aniston then, and he wasn't interested in meeting girls. When me and the other guys went out without him, girls would come up to us, angling for an introduction to Vince. "You were so funny tonight," they'd say.

"Thanks."

"Yeah, you were really great."

"Thanks, again," we'd say, hopes rising.

"So is Vince with you guys tonight?"

Hopes dashed.

That wasn't always the case. There were times when fans came up to me, Bret, John, and Ahmed, just to meet and hang out with us. But a lot of times, they were just working us to get to Vince. And I can't say that we blew off these women after we figured out their true intentions. There were many late nights out on the tour, partying and meeting new people. We ate ribs in Oklahoma, tacos in Texas, pulled pork in Kentucky, and cheesy chili in Wisconsin, sampling the specialty hot dishes wherever we went.

But no matter how late you were out, you had to be back on the bus by curfew, or you'd have to pay your own way to the next gig. So, if the bus left Alabama at 2 a.m., and you missed it talking to a girl at a bar, you would have to rent a car or hitchhike to the next city. I never missed curfew, because I didn't want to be the troublemaker. I did cut it close a few times, though.

Vince got up every single morning at five or six to do radio interviews to promote the next gig. I remember the publicist coming on the bus at dawn, saying, "Vince, we've got a call." He'd take the phone into the parking lot and do seven radio station spots back to back. There was no ad or promotional budget for the tour. The only way to publicize the gigs was for Vince to get on the phone and be funny on the radio. Drive time listeners learned that he'd be in their town tomorrow night, and they'd buy tickets. Our shows would sell out on the power of those radio spots alone. I listened to him many mornings, putting the same energy and enthusiasm into each interview and never begging off, no matter how tired or hungover he might be. I thought, *Okay, so this is how it works.* You have to sell tickets. You have to convince people to come out, spend money, and give you a night of their lives. The work you do before the show is as important as the work you do at the show.

A lot of comedians don't want to put in the time or get out of bed to sell tickets to their own shows, as if people will know who they are by magic. My take-away from watching Vince in action was that the big stars are big for a reason. They have the work ethic. They care enough about what they're doing to make it a success. Ever since that tour, I have followed his example and done whatever I can to promote. And after the show, for years to come, I would hang out in the lobby of the venue and shake hands with anyone in the audience who wanted to meet me. As I got more well known, it would take hours, and I was happy to do it. If you'd been playing gigs for ten years without anyone remembering your name after the show, when you finally connected with fans, you'd want to shake hands and thank every one of them, too.

AT THE TIME, Bret and John had development deals with major networks. Ahmed toured nationally and internationally and he ran comedy rooms. During an interview for the documentary film about the tour, Bret made a comment that I was where the other guys were five years ago, making it sound like I was the comedy novice to their grisly veterans. But the truth is, we had all started out around the same time. No one had years on me, but they had gotten farther than me. I think that only made me more grateful to be with them, their equal on tour.

There was no jealousy or one-upmanship on the bus. Not a lot of shoptalk either. We didn't discuss the art of comedy or compare notes about our careers so far. The vibe was more like a fraternity. When you're in college, you don't talk about getting a job when you graduate. You just have fun and live in the moment. That was how it felt on the Wild West Show. I avoided talking about what would happen when it was over. Most likely, I was going back to the penguin suit. I hoped the cachet of this tour would lead to better-paying gigs for me, but I'd thought that before and been disappointed. I put my future fears aside for thirty days and concentrated on having a great time with those guys, doing comedy at those venues, sleeping and living on the bus. I knew it was a once-in-a-lifetime experience that I would probably never repeat. Looking back, my memories of the Wild West Comedy Show are only golden. It was a constant stream of fun. I knew a return to the Four Seasons loomed when it was over, but I pushed that to the back of my mind and really soaked up every day like it was my last.

And then the last day came.

The final performance was in my hometown (and Vince's). I had my family and friends there. Returning to Chicago with Vince Vaughn and making my parents proud of me was a watershed moment. We'd had some shaky exchanges when they expressed doubt about my career choice. Now, for the first time in seven years, my parents had a sense that I was on the right track. The documentary director Ari Sandel, an Oscar winner for the short film *West Bank Story*, interviewed my parents. My father said, "He's going to make it. I don't know when, but he's going to make it." It all came together for me that night—the vote of confidence from my family, the excitement of my friends, the bonds I'd made on the road with the other comedians and the crew. I felt deeply connected to everyone in my life that night.

And then, it was over.

We did a final interview for Ari, talking about what the tour meant for us and how we felt about it coming to an end. Of course, I got emotional, and unsuccessfully fought back tears, saying, "I'm kind of choked up because it's . . . uh . . . a lot of emotion going on. I don't want to be a pussy or nothing. I loved every minute of this, man, and I just don't want it to end." They all reached out with a shoulder squeeze. I really did love those guys. I was overwhelmed by the experience, the friendships, the adventure. The joy poured out through my tear ducts. It had nowhere else to go.

That fit of sentimentality would come back to haunt me three years later, when *Wild West Comedy Show: 30 Days & 30 Nights—Hollywood to the Heartland* was finally released in theaters. My parents and friends flew to L.A. for the premiere. When my buddies saw the crying scene, they sank in their seats. Out of all of them, I'm the most emotional, but they'd never seen me cry before.

At the after party, they tore me to shreds about it. From that day on, the phrase "I don't want to be a pussy or nothing . . ." has come up in conversation with them. Then my buddies start laughing at me so hard, the tears run down their faces.

And I say, "Who's crying now, motherfuckers?"

I MADE SOME money on the tour, about five grand. It was more than I would have made at the Four Seasons in a month by far. I decided that, with this cushion, I didn't have to rush back there. I gave myself permission not to. The next month, I landed a corporate gig at a sales conference in L.A. I got $3,500 for that, so now my cushion was growing.

On top of that, I had newfound credibility with comedy club owners because of the Vince Vaughn seal of approval. Being tapped to be on his tour was good enough for them. Seeing an opportunity, I suggested to my agent, "Why don't we see if we can shore up a gig at a comedy club in Dallas?" I'd just been there on the tour, and my name was fresh in their minds. I figured the owners would think, *Let's see what this guy's got on his own.*

I'd had a taste of the "all comedy, all the time" life, and I wanted more. "Whatever work comes in, I'll take it," I said to my agent. "I don't care if it's a week in the sticks, six shows, three on Saturday, whatever it is, I'll do it." Miraculously, the calls did come in, with me as a headliner. Before long, I was back on the road, doing gigs all over the country, begging off shifts at the Four Seasons every week.

After a year of this, the manager at the lounge called me and said, "Listen, we need to know if you're ever coming back to work. Because if you're not, we need the locker space."

This was it, what I consider a turning point in my life and career. If I held on to that locker, I'd have a safety net. If the gigs dried up, I'd have somewhere to go and a way to earn a living. Or, I could quit the day job, go hard on the comedy circuit, and continue to build a fan base and improve my act. It would be a risk. In my eight years on the edges of the comedy world, I'd seen guys with huge potential and big crowds flame out or burn out. I'd also seen people who would dip their toe in halfway, and never put everything they had into it.

It was an easy decision to make. Took about five seconds.

I told the Four Seasons manager, "I'm not coming back. Whatever is in my locker, just give it away."

My locker was small, a half locker on the bottom row. I had no idea what was in there, probably some spare change, a couple pens, and a pair of worn-out work shoes. I never invested in good shoes, probably a mistake for someone on his feet for eight hours a day. The heel of my shoe would often be loose. It would flop around like a flip-flop but it still worked.

I think those cheap shoes fucked up my feet permanently. But better shoes would have been a kind of defeat, like resigning myself to being a waitress for the rest of my life. Any money I made was spent on doing comedy and paying back my father.

Beat-up shoes and flat feet didn't stop me from making the biggest leap of faith so far in my life. On September 12, 2006, I left the job that had supported my dream for eight years. I took a gamble, and this time, it paid off.

6

HUNGRY HEART

By late 2008, I'd been doing comedy in L.A. for over a decade. Thanks to my associations with Dice and Vince, I had enough clout to book comedy clubs all over the country. I even did a tour in the Middle East (Saudi Arabia, Lebanon, Qatar, and Egypt) with Ahmed Ahmed and some other guys. I was working full-time as a comedian, having some degree of success, and making a decent living. I was in a nice place professionally.

Personally? Romantically? I was nowhere.

In all my time in L.A., I had dated here and there, but nothing serious. Before the ball started rolling with my comedy, I didn't have enough money to take someone out. And once I was coming up, I traveled fifty-two weekends out of the year.

I was focused on my career. It sounds like an L.A. douche bag thing to say: "I'm too busy for a relationship!" But I was *always* on the road. I would leave town on Wednesday and come back on Monday, every single week. What woman would be okay with that? I had to take the work to make money and build my reputation.

The only long-term relationship I had while living in L.A. was with a woman in Dallas. I met her while on the Wild West tour, but she hadn't come to my show. Me and the other guys went to a bar afterward and I met her there. We had a great time talking and laughing that night, and we started to write emails and texts to each other. Then we started having actual phone conversations. A year went by and we evolved into traveling to see each other; either she came to L.A. for a few days or I went to Dallas. She was a nice girl, funny and cool. The slow pace and distance between us allowed us to get to know one another in an old-fashioned way, by writing and talking. We had a good time together, but I kind of always knew that it wasn't going to go further, for a few reasons, only one of which was our living in two different states. After four years, I decided that there was no point in continuing, so we ended it.

My life didn't change dramatically after that breakup, but it felt different to be single. Part of the reason the long-distance relationship had worked for me for so long was that it took the pressure off. I didn't have to look too closely at how I'd organized my life to prevent a serious connection from developing.

It wasn't like I woke up and said, "Seb, you're thirty-five. You've never had a committed relationship in your entire adult life. It's time." But I did feel a shift in how I was thinking about what my next relationship would be like. For starters, she would have to live in L.A.

I put out some feelers for fix-ups to one of my best friends (also my personal trainer), John Petrelli. John and I met on the set of *Days of Our Lives* doing extra work in 1998. We were on a lunch break and we began talking. I'd never met anybody more annoyed at the world than myself. He's from upstate New York, from an Italian family, a great guy who'd take the shirt off his back for you, and we hit it off immediately. He comes across like the Ultimate Man. Hunts his own food. Does jujitsu. He's a martial artist, a builder, a fisherman, and a survivalist. You could drop him in the woods naked with a piece of string and a toothpick, and he'd emerge a week later, well fed and wearing a bear skin. In other words, John is the total opposite of me.

I asked him, "Do you train any good-looking women?"

He said, "Actually, I have one, but she comes early, around 7 a.m."

I usually had my session at the gym at ten, but I said, "All right, schedule me right after her so I can see what she looks like."

Yes, I plotted with John to scope out a complete stranger. He made her sound pretty and funny, and I just wanted to meet her. I thought I couldn't be too obvious about it, or she'd be turned off immediately. It had to seem organic, almost accidental—and I had to look my best. Even though I was showing up at the gym first thing in the morning, when most people were just rolling out of bed into their workout clothes, I got up at 6 a.m. to do a full body prep—hair, skin, nails, shave. I may have gotten a little over-involved with the grooming, like I was doing a bodybuilding competition, and not a casual workout on a Tuesday.

I showed up around 7:55, right at the end of her session, as John and I had planned. He said, "Hey, Sebastian. Five minutes early. I love it. Lana and I are just finishing up. Lana, this is my old friend Sebastian. Sebastian, this is my client Lana."

Lana and I shook hands and said "Nice to meet you," and then she left.

Once she was out of earshot, John asked, "So?"

"She's cute."

Really cute. Blond, petite, with a smile that lit up the room; sweet, friendly, with a surprising Southern accent. I learned later she grew up in Memphis, Tennessee.

I was about to ask him how to proceed to get to know her better, when John put a damper on it. "She has a boyfriend," he said.

Oh, well. That changed things. We talked about it while training. John started stretching me out, pushing my leg to one side, and his fingers slid right off my skin. "Why the hell are you so greasy, man?" he asked.

"It's baby oil."

"You put baby oil on your legs at seven in the morning to make a good impression on a girl?"

In hindsight, it does seem ridiculous. I asked Lana years later if she noticed how sexy and shiny my legs were when we first met. She nodded and said, "I just thought you were so out of shape that you were sweaty before you even began working out."

I wasn't going to move in on her if she had a boyfriend, but over the next few weeks, John hinted to me that he didn't think that Lana and Mr. X were going to last. Apparently, they had met at the University of Tennessee and come to L.A. together, but there was trouble in paradise. I told John to let me know if they broke up, which they did a few months later, but then she took up with some other guy. John delivered the intel: "Good news! Lana broke up with the college boyfriend. Bad news! She's seeing someone else."

In December, I started seeing Lana around the gym by accident for real. She'd switched to 9 a.m. training sessions, and I was at my usual 10 a.m. slot. When we crossed paths, we'd say, "Hey, how you doing?" I would throw in a compliment or whatnot, something like, "Your hair looks good today." She would say, "Thanks," always polite, but she gave me no sign of interest. She remembers me saying once, "You look like you lost some weight," and she replied, "Oh, I guess I was fat before." I was just saying anything to start up a conversation, but in hindsight, that's not something you should say to a lady.

I decided to ask her out anyway. I told John what I was going to do, and he sussed her out about it with the subtlety of a sledgehammer.

"My client Sebastian wants to take you on a date," he said.

This information came out of nowhere for her. Although I'd been complimenting her and smiling hard for weeks, she had no idea I was flirting until John said something. She replied to John, "Tell Sebastian I don't date anybody who has a higher body fat percentage than me."

She was joking (her comedy is so dry). All of John's clients had just had their body fat tested, and she knew that there was no way mine was less than hers. Next time I saw her, I got on the treadmill next to her, started running alongside, and said, "Word has it that you don't date anybody with more than twenty percent body fat. I don't fall into that category. I could get there eventually, but in the meantime, would you like to go out to dinner with me?"

Lana laughed and said, "Okay." We decided on Sushi Roku on Third Street in L.A.

Right on time, I picked her up at her place, a really cute house. She opened the door and said, "I'm still getting ready. Come on in."

I went in, expecting to wait in the living room or kitchen for her to finish, maybe meet her roommates or something. But she brought me right into the bedroom and told me to have a seat on the bed while she put on her makeup right in front of me.

I might've said, "Okay, we just met."

It just felt too friendly, too intimate, too soon. There wasn't the barrier that should have been up, or at least had always been up, on first dates with other women. Normally, you don't get that peek behind the curtain right away. Lana's complete lack of mystery had me baffled. I know now that my wife has a resting smile face, but that night, her grin had an edge. Apparently, I made her nervous, and yet she'd invited me into her bedroom after thirty seconds.

Another thing that confused me: She didn't have roommates. The whole house was hers. She was barely out of college and she had her own home? I thought, *What's going on here?* It was no dump, either. The house was quaint, artsy, full of paintings, sculptures, eclectic objects, shelves full of books, crystal jobbies, a painted chalkboard with doodles and drawings, cool lighting fixtures. The whole place was beautifully designed, with custom-made furniture. The vintage chairs were different from the upholstered couch, with mismatched decorative pillows, like they had been picked out separately.

Where I grew up, you went to Wickes Furniture and just bought the complete set.

John had warned me that Lana's family was well off, but until I saw her house, I didn't know the extent. When I was twenty-five, I was in a dark one-bedroom in full view of a couch humper.

So we came from different worlds. That was okay. I'd met all kinds of people since I moved to L.A. I wasn't worried about her background or intimidated by it. It just added another layer of intrigue. I wanted to hear more about growing up down South, which I knew nothing about, and how she had decided to move to L.A. I could tell her my stories about Chicago. We'd have a lot to talk about.

But as soon as we got in my car to drive to the restaurant, she stopped talking.

We sat down at the table, and still, she didn't speak. Not even to say what she wanted to eat. I ordered for us both. Throughout the entire meal, I did *all* the talking. She was polite and engaged, always smiling. But there was nothing coming out of her mouth. I ran through a ninety-minute extended monologue. It was agony. I even dipped into doing my act, on the first date, to fill the time.

I could tell she was nervous or shy beyond belief. But why? It wasn't like we hadn't spoken to each other before. I'd just been in her bedroom! After sushi, we went to Pinkberry at the Grove—an outdoor shopping mall. She still didn't talk, but it was easier to not have a conversation while walking around in a crowded place. By the time I dropped her off, I'd completely run out of material.

The next day, John asked me, "How'd it go?"

I said, "She didn't speak."

"Lana? Lana Gomez? *What!?* I can't get her to shut up."

"Yeah, well, she's a sweet girl," I said. "Really nice, polite, but not much to say."

After thinking about it for a week, I chalked up her silence to extreme shyness or nerves. It was worth trying again. I called her and she told me she was at work. She was an artist, the resident painter at the Kelly Wearstler Boutique, her favorite interior design company in L.A. She was getting her feet wet and learning from Kelly, a woman Lana admired who was and still is one of her biggest inspirations.

We had a fantastic chat on the phone, with some great banter. So why was she so quiet face-to-face? Then she admitted, "I'd never been on a first date before."

At the time, Lana was twenty-five, and she'd been a serial monogamist. She and her friends would all go out to parties together. Socializing was more communal. They would go out to a bar or to somebody's house with sixteen people. Her generation didn't date per se. They hung out.

That was not how I rolled. I loved dating, especially first dates. I'd been on dozens of them, Mr. I'll-Take-You-Out-We'll-Have-A-Nice-Dinner-And-A-Cocktail-After. The first proper date Lana had ever been on—when a guy picked her up, took her to dinner, and brought her home—was with me.

She added, "I was intimidated. All I know about you is what I found on Google."

Pre-date Googling, the curse of the digital age.

She'd read some interviews with me and found videos on YouTube.

Not good. Since Lana was so silent, I was drawing straws and had gone into my act in order to have any conversation, and she had just watched the clips earlier that day on the computer. She had seen how critical of other people I was in my comedy, and she was afraid she'd say or do something that I'd be offended by or would judge harshly. She didn't want to give me material that would later turn up in my act.

The irony is, now I get material from her constantly, and she's in my act every night.

"I was shy," she said. "I have no idea why. I'm never like that!"

We kept talking, and I started to tune into her deadpan sarcasm and dry humor over the phone, and I was really liking it.

ON OUR NEXT date, we went to see *Frost/Nixon* with Frank Langella and Michael Sheen. It was a weird choice for a second date. The movie wasn't a formulaic romantic comedy, although Frost and Nixon butted heads in the beginning and got together by the end (kind of). The whole time, I was worried about what Lana and I were going to talk about after. Lana wasn't born until nine years after Nixon resigned. She barely knew anything about him. I suggested the movie because I like historical films, but in hindsight, maybe I should have picked something even remotely sexy. I could tell that I needed to implement something fun to get the night going, so we got margaritas after the movie and the conversation flowed well.

On our third date, we went on a hike to Runyon Canyon. Lana had told me that she'd been a competitive gymnast throughout high school. I'd seen her on the treadmill at the gym, and I knew she was in incredible shape, not to mention ten years younger than me. And I was . . . doing my best. I wasn't in *bad* shape (just ask John Travolta), but I'm more of an indoor kind of person generally.

When you first start dating, you want to feel like you can impress the girl. As we hiked up the mountain, I quickly realized that was not going to happen. I didn't have the stamina to keep up with her. At one point, she grabbed my hand. While trying not to overtly gasp for breath, I had the presence of mind to think, *Oh, how sweet. She wants to hold hands.* My heart beat a little faster, which is saying a lot.

But then she said, "Come *on!*" She wasn't being romantic. She grabbed my hand to tug me along faster.

Lana wasn't going to slow down for me, and she expected me to pick up the pace. This dynamic—her pushing me (or pulling me) to push myself—has been a recurring theme in our relationship. When I grew up, I did some things (homework, school projects) half-assed. I put effort into things I cared about, like my style, but otherwise, I was okay with okay.

133

Not Lana. She puts extra effort into everything, from hiking a mountain to wrapping a gift to raising our daughter. She's a born perfectionist with an eye for detail. I might look at, say, a hotel room, and think, *It's all right*. But Lana will dissect it, and say, "The color is off. The couch makes no sense over here." After nine years together, now I, too, walk into a room and notice five things I'd change to improve it. In a way, Lana has made me *even more judgmental*. In my single life, I asked, "How can I make it?" In my married life, I ask, "How can I make it better?" Before that Runyon Canyon hike, I never would have imagined I could practically run up a mountain. I'm not a perfectionist like she is, by any means, but when I watch her work extra hard at the gym or go the extra mile in any arena of life, I feel like I have to try to match her, or I'll never catch up.

When we got to the top of the mountain that day, I looked at her and she looked at me. I was gasping, dizzy and sweaty. Then I saw the Holy Grail, a water fountain! I ran over and took a big sip. Then I looked behind me and realized there was a line of people . . . holding dogs. Lana smiled sweetly as she said, "Oh my God. I can't believe you drank out of the fountain where the dogs all drink."

We didn't kiss that day, or on our fourth date. Or the fifth or sixth.

I definitely, desperately, wanted to kiss her, but I was still getting to know her and her sense of humor. She wasn't demonstrably affectionate and never gave me any obvious cues that said, "Kiss me now!" She kept saying yes to dates, but I wasn't sure how she felt about me. I asked myself, *Does she even like me? Where are we going with this?*

Lana could run a mile in eight minutes flat, but the pace of our relationship was agonizingly slow. To be honest with you, it was strange for me. I'd never waited seven dates to kiss someone in my life. But for whatever reason, lunging in, mouth open, didn't feel like the right thing to do with her. I was waiting for the right moment.

About a month into our whatever-it-was, we were at her house, hanging out on the couch, talking. It was getting late. I was going to Dubai the next day and had to go home to pack, so I said, "I've got to go."

She said, "Okay."

We made eye contact, held it, and without words or any nonverbal communication, we leaned toward each other and kissed for the first time. It was a passionate kiss, but I understood it wasn't going any farther. Clothes were not going to come flying off. After a few minutes, we separated and said goodbye.

In my car, driving home, I was reeling. *What just happened? Does that mean we're together? So she* does *like me?* I could not figure her out. To this day, there are moments when my wife mystifies me. Keeps things interesting.

The Dubai trip was an all-expenses-paid five-day gig to perform at a wedding. The groom's father—a real estate mogul in

India—was paying me $15,000 for one night's work. It was the most I'd been paid in my career. They'd originally wanted Russell Peters, an Indian comedian, but he wasn't available or he asked for too much. I guess I was next on their list, and I jumped at the opportunity.

I'd just had a breakthrough with Lana, though, and leaving town immediately after didn't feel right. Although the timing wasn't ideal, I somehow managed to enjoy the unlimited champagne and flat-bed seat in my first class cabin, also paid for by the groom's father. The flight attendants on Emirates wear those adorable little red hats with the white veil, and they're always smiling. They were nothing like the flight attendants on American Airlines, who look at you like they want to kill you for asking for a blanket.

After the seventeen-hour flight, I was picked up in a limo and taken to the Burj Al Arab Jumeira, aka "The Most Luxurious Hotel in the World." It looks like a sailboat in the sky. I was shown into a luxury suite with panoramic views of Dubai, and introduced to my private butler. It was so over-the-top opulent. Everything was silk or crystal. There was a mirror over the bed. The Burj Al Arab is called a seven-star hotel. There's no such thing. They just made that up to sound unrivaled. I, for one, had never seen anything like this before. It was kind of gaudy, to be honest. Lavish, but also tacky.

The wedding planner came by to check on me, and told me about all the activities planned for guests throughout the weekend. Dune buggy rides, surfing school on artificial waves, hot air ballooning. I listened to the list of my options, but all I could think was *If only Lana were here.* When a relationship is just starting to kick off, you want to be joined at the hip, to share everything. In that phase of love, going food shopping at Ralph's is a crazy fun adventure. And here I was, in an exotic location, living in insane luxury, but it felt empty. We weren't even two months in, and I missed her already.

I passed on the dune buggies and surfing. I didn't know anyone and I hate to be the fifth wheel. The idea of showing up at some activity with the wedding guests mouthing "Who's this guy?" to each other was enough to keep me away. Besides that, I don't like to interact with the audience before I do comedy. When I have corporate gigs, the organizers often ask me to sit down for a dinner with the company's staff beforehand. But I can't eat a plate of chicken and rice, make small talk with strangers, and then say "excuse me" and go on stage.

Whether it's a high school auditorium or a Broadway theater, the audience is separated from the actors with a curtain. It creates a divide between reality and the willful illusion of the show. You don't want to see the actors putting on their makeup and costumes beforehand. To enjoy the experience of the show, you need to believe that the stage is another world.

I feel the same way about comedy. Mingling with the audience or even walking through the casino before a show spoils the mystery. I want the audience to think I was air-dropped onto the stage, like, "How'd he get here?" Going on a camel ride with the wedding guests beforehand would have ruined it.

The only perk I took my hosts up on was a massage. Even then, I didn't feel comfortable taking advantage. I got the fifty-minute basic rubdown instead of the hour-and-a-half four-handed hot rock aromatherapy treatment with the bells and whistles. I kept thinking they'd look at the bill and say, "The fucking comedian got an hour-and-a-half massage?" In truth, they probably wouldn't have cared or even noticed. I could have had spa treatments dawn to dusk and no one would've batted an eye. I felt guilty about using the butler. My first night, he asked, "Would you like me to draw you a bath?" What would that entail? Turning on the faucet and putting some soap in there? What the hell was he going to do? I declined that, too. I drew my own bath, and I shoveled all the Hermès bath products into my suitcase.

I spent much of that weekend alone in my suite or at the pool by myself, but I wasn't lonely. I was communicating with Lana the whole time. Of course, it would have been much more fun if she had actually been there, but it sufficed to send her photos and videos with "Holy shit, will you look at this!" captions. The way my wife grew up, she'd seen luxury hotels and was very well traveled. She even did Semester at Sea in college, studying on a ship for a few months, visiting ten different countries. She'd gone to Cambodia in college. The farthest I'd gotten was Cancun. I don't think she had the same shock and awe reaction to the Burj Al Arab that I did, but she had never been there and was loving my updates.

Being in that otherworldly place, performing at a wedding, made me think of all the meals and vacations I hoped to have one day with a wife and family. Since Lana was on my mind, I put her in the role of bride. I'd never done that before, with any girlfriend. We'd only just kissed once, and it was way too early to go there mentally. But instead of being scared, I liked what I imagined. I could see it with her.

When I got home, the slow pace of our relationship suddenly hit the gas. We were together constantly, spending most nights at her place. Every Saturday I was in town, we'd lie out all day by her pool. At night, we'd try every restaurant in the city. I went from *Does she even like me?* to falling in love in just a few weeks. What had finally brought us together was being 8,300 miles apart.

LANA AND I had been an official couple for about two months when she told me her mother and stepfather were coming to L.A. from their home in Naples, Florida, and they wanted to meet me.

She'd previously described her large, blended family. Barry, Lana's father, had passed away suddenly, tragically, when she was seventeen. A few years later, her mother, Simone, married Scott. Simone had been married before Barry, and had two kids from that marriage, Lana's half brother and half sister. Scott had also been married before Simone, and had four children from that marriage. Although Lana was the only child of Simone and Barry, she had two half siblings and four stepsiblings, along with nine (half/step) nieces and nephews. Serafina, our baby daughter, already has a *lot* of cousins.

I didn't grow up with a large or blended family. The Maniscalcos of Arlington Heights, Illinois, are a small clan, and we're full blood related. My parents were only married to each other (until that ended unexpectedly several years ago). My sister is my sister, no qualifiers. We're all Catholic. Lana's Jewish, but some of her siblings aren't. I needed a chart to figure all this out.

As complicated as her family was, everyone got along. They were close like my family. The feelings were the same, even if their Brady Bunch circumstances were wildly different.

Meeting her parents was a major step, one I had rarely taken with any girlfriend before. I knew how close Lana was with her mom and her stepfather, and how important it was for me to win their approval. She downplayed the upcoming meeting, but it was a big deal. The key to making a good impression was to find common ground. How was I, a middle-class Italian guy from Illinois, going to connect with Lana's golf-loving wealthy parents from Florida? They might be stuck-up snobs and look down on me and my background. Or they might be warm and accepting. I had no idea. All I knew was that if they didn't like me, it could be a deal breaker.

The plan was to have dinner at Chinois on Main, Wolfgang Puck's restaurant in Santa Monica. Nowadays, Chinois is one of our favorite restaurants, but at that time, it was new to me. Everything was new. New relationship, new restaurant, new potential in-laws. They offered to pick me up, but as a man, I could not accept the offer. I had to meet them there. I don't like talking to people from the backseat. You can't see their faces, or gauge how they're reacting. It's just not ideal. I wanted to engage them in conversation while seated across a table. It was the way I preferred to do it. I also wore my glasses because I thought they would make me look more intelligent. Scott, her stepdad, went to Stanford, for God's sake.

First impression (mine): Simone was funny, sweet, and easy to get along with. Scott came off as impatient, gruff, the type of guy who with one glance in your direction telegraphs, "Get to the point already." My family style is to tell stories the long way, to be loud and expressive with lots of commentary and banter. We just sit around and go, "So what else is going on?" Casual. Scott can't take more than twenty-two words at a time. Lana was really good with him, though, loosening up his straight-laced intensity with her sarcasm.

Scott asked for the wine list. He intended to buy a bottle.

At the time, I was a "by the glass" guy. My friends and I never ordered bottles or even specified winemakers. You wanted a glass of wine, you ordered a glass.

As I've come to learn, Scott is referred to as the "Grape

Ape" because he's like an encyclopedia of good wines. Wine lists themselves intimidated the hell out of me. The menu is leather-bound, the paper is heavy stock. At some restaurants, the wine list is so enormous, they bring it out on a pedestal, with a reverent hush. The sommelier is a priest and the wine list is the Holy Book with a tassel as a bookmark.

As Scott perused the Chinois list, I said a little prayer that I could afford whatever the Grape Ape picked out. I went into this dinner thinking that I'd pay for the meal. I wanted to do my part as the host in L.A., and as the man who was trying to impress his girlfriend's parents. So Scott ordered a bottle of French wine with a long name, and then started rattling off menu items to the waiter so quickly, I couldn't add up the prices fast enough in my head.

"To start," he said, "we'll have the spring rolls, the Chinese chicken salad, the Szechuan pancakes, the ribs, and, for entrées, the duck, the sea bass, the pork shoulder, sizzling catfish . . ."

And I'm thinking, *Oh my God. Did I bring enough money for that?*

He ordered so much food, it was staggering. The knot of cash in my pocket wouldn't even cover the appetizers. I thought, *I'll pay for the wine at least.* But could I? Scott held the wine list, so I couldn't see the prices. I devised a plan of going to the bathroom, snagging a wine list on the way, finding the bottle he ordered, and checking if I had enough cash to cover it.

Despite my anxiety, we had a nice dinner. Lana's parents

didn't carry themselves like snobs. They were just good people who loved food and wine. Lana was constantly smiling and touching my leg under the table, letting me know she was happy about how things were going.

When the bill came—the equivalent of a month's rent for me—I swallowed hard and said, "Can I contribute?"

Scott said, "Absolutely not. It's done," and then he changed the subject. I saw his credit card come back to the table with the bill already paid. He must have slipped it to the waiter beforehand (I found this to be the ultimate gentleman's trick and have since implemented it in my repertoire). And his card wasn't plastic. It was titanium or something. The material of the credit card itself was worth more than my savings account.

I was so relieved by how he'd handled the bill, I decided that Scott was a good guy. He was brisk but generous and he was excited to teach me about wine. He's lived up to that promise, and spoiled me rotten. Up to this point, I'd go to the grocery store and pick the $9.99 Pinot Noir. Wine didn't have a story, it just had a color, red or white. My father-in-law introduced me to a world of wine that I'd never really known existed. He educated me about the characteristics of wine, and how much to pour in a glass (not all the way to the top). I didn't know that wine had to breathe. Who the hell knew that wine breathes; does it have a nose? I also didn't know that it's a cardinal sin not to make eye contact while toasting. People say that sound is the only sense that isn't used when drinking wine. You smell, taste, see, feel, but the reason you clink your glasses is so the damn thing goes full circle. There is sound! You must make eye contact to complete the sensory experience, and you better believe that I do the eye thing because urban legend says if you don't do this, you will have bad sex for seven years. Through Scott, wine became a conduit for me to learn about weather, cultures, families, and heritage. Ask me what year Napoleon fought the battle of Waterloo, I have absolutely no idea. But ask me the best year for a California Cabernet—1996, baby!

Anyway, later that night, Lana and I summed up our Chinois dinner in bed. "They liked you," she said. "And what's with the glasses?"

THAT FALL, LANA and I went to her parents' in Naples for Thanksgiving. I was under a tremendous amount of work stress—touring, management changes—and worried about yet another milestone in our relationship. I'd met the parents already. But now I was going to meet everyone else—the siblings, their spouses and kids, aunts, uncles, family friends. They'd all be checking me out. Even though Simone and Scott had been great in L.A., I was concerned that the difference in our backgrounds would be even more obvious on their turf. Going to their home on the Gulf Coast, right on the water, to be scrutinized by dozens of strangers—and sit for an hours-long formal family dinner—triggered my anxiety. In my family, dinner seating is general admission. In Lana's you're assigned seats like at a wedding. If I hadn't been crazy in love with her, I wouldn't have gone. We hadn't said the words yet, though I was bursting to do it.

A few weeks before the holiday, I was doing a gig in Branson, Missouri. I got up in the morning, went to the bathroom to brush my teeth, opened my mouth, and saw a horror.

My tongue had some type of topography map on it written in white fungus. It was covered with white shapes on the top and sides.

I thought I was dying and my tongue was the first thing to pass away. I don't know what was worse, that I was going to be passing away, or that my final hours would be in Branson, Missouri. I didn't want to die there, so I canceled my show (one of two times I've ever done that; the other was for my daughter's birth). I landed in L.A., and my sister, a longtime Californian by then, met me at the emergency room. Once I got in to see a doctor, he informed me it was a condition called "geographic tongue," probably brought on by stress. Hearing that it was harmless and would go away on its own didn't fill me with comfort. I was constantly looking in the mirror, and every time, I would get all worked up again.

My tongue was still white as paste when we boarded our flight for Florida. I was blown away by Lana's parents' house in Naples. The place was huge, as expected, and beautiful. It was not like anything I'd been exposed to before. It had a comfortable feel, but high-styled, decorated and artful. I could see where Lana got her taste.

I smiled with tightly closed lips when I was introduced to the rest of her family, making sure no one saw my tongue. I was worried people would think, *The comedian doesn't smile much, does he?*

Lana and I were put in a separate little guest home, also comfortable-yet-elegant. Simone had left an article from the newspaper about standup comedy on the bed. I came to learn that she was always thoughtful like that, clipping articles and sending small gifts. One part of my brain was going, *People take the time to do this shit?* The other part really appreciated the kindness. Simone made me feel welcomed and accepted. So accepted, she wasn't even disgusted by my fuzzy tongue. She knew I was sick and made some Cornish hens stuffed with wild rice, a home-cooked meal that was the perfect remedy to make me feel better.

The next day, I woke up, went to the bathroom to brush my teeth, opened my mouth, and saw a healthy, pink tongue.

Jewish penicillin worked! A Cornish hen saved my life. I smiled normally at dinner. Everyone talked over one another, and though I was used to a captive audience, with one person speaking at a time and others listening, I proceeded to get the seal of approval from all of Lana's relatives, blood, half-blood, and no-blood.

YOU MIGHT BE thinking, *What about* your *family?*

The tables were turned at Christmas, when I brought Lana to my mom's house in Chicago. My parents were recently separated, and the family was adjusting to that. No more holiday celebrations in my childhood home on the corner lot.

I immersed Lana in the Chicago experience. She hung out around the kitchen table with my family. I had all my friends over. It was a total onslaught for her, but she handled it well. When you take somebody to your hometown, you want to show them where you go to eat, what you like. I grew up on Portillo's hot dogs and hamburgers, so that was one of our first stops. She sampled a classic Chicago dog (onion, mustard, relish, and a pickle) and an enormous charbroiled burger, and she loved it all. I loved the fact that Lana enjoyed eating food from my hometown, and we had a blast laughing while I shared stories of my childhood with my people.

I gave her a day to rest her stomach, and then we went to Johnnie's Beef. In Chicago, Italian beef sandwiches with peppers and juice are *the thing*. She'd never had one before, and Johnnie's, an all-cash joint on Arlington Heights Road, makes the best. I ordered a sandwich with beef and giardiniera peppers as well as fries, hoping she'd like it as much as I do. She absolutely loved every bite. Watching her enjoy the nostalgic places from my childhood made them new for me again.

She said to me, "I like it here. Good stuff, good people." My heart sang.

Back home, we went out to shovel snow off the driveway. I was bursting to tell her that I loved her, and I intended to do it that night. While I was shoveling, I saw her making letters in the snow. I looked over to read her message. She'd written in huge letters, "LANA ♥ SEBASTIAN."

It was kind of high school, kind of goofy, but that was what I loved about Lana. She's got an innocent quality that I find cute and endearing. I think all artists have to retain the wonder of a child in order to create. I tend to be cynical and anxious, but then she does something like professing her love in the snow, and all my stress just drains out of me.

So she said it first. Or, she wrote it first.

I said it back, and that was it. From that moment on, we were inseparable. When I wasn't touring, I was with her. She started to come to my local gigs, and whenever possible, she went out on tour with me. I went from being the lone ranger to a guy who was smitten. We could do anything together—work out, eat, explore, cry (well, I'm the crier, she's not), or go to CVS—and we were always laughing and having a good time.

I CONTINUED TO move up in comedy, doing specials and standup gigs for larger crowds. Lana's career was flourishing as well. Kelly Wearstler published a design book called *Hue* that featured a picture of a huge ten-by-twelve-foot painting of Lana's. Since Kelly is very well respected, her giving Lana that validation inspired even more people to call Lana to commission paintings. She was tapped to create public artworks in the city of L.A. Eventually, Lana turned 100 percent of her focus on pursuing her own projects. We're still friends with Kelly. She just did the interiors at our home and converted our garage into an incredible art studio.

After two years, I moved in with Lana. Another year went by, and I gave up the lease on my one-bedroom. We both love to travel and wanted to see the world together. We just kind of bounced around for a while, going to Italy, Australia, Mexico, and Napa. We talked about next steps and always knew we'd get married and have kids, but there didn't seem to be any rush. We finally got married on August 24, 2013, four and a half years after our first date.

We decided to have the wedding in Napa. We had a connection to the region, having taken our first vacation in wine country with Lana's parents. We did a hot air balloon ride and really kind of fell in love with the quaint little restaurants up there, the vineyards, the food, the wine, the environment. We knew early on we wanted to do a destination wedding—not Chicago, not Naples. It didn't seem right to have it on one person's home turf. We lived in California, so we would get married here. And if our guests wanted to come, we'd make it worth their while.

We were adults when we married—I was forty and Lana was thirty—so we didn't really need things. I was against a registry anyway. I used to do a bit about Italian weddings:

Italians don't register at Bed, Bath & Beyond. You don't bring a toaster to a wedding. Italians bring cash. We put it in an envelope. Sometimes, there's not even a card. We put it in the envelope with a Post-it note: "Congrats!" The bride and groom know they're getting cash. They're sitting here with a satin bag that says "CASH" bedazzled in rhinestones. And people walk in and they start making a deposit. Some people wait. They have the dinner, eating the chicken. "Chicken's kind of dry. The food stinks. Take a hundred out of the envelope."

For me, coming from where I come from, there's no wedding planner. *You* plan the wedding. *You* hire the caterer. *You* pick the flowers. *You* find a place to rent tables and whatnot. And by "you," I do not mean "me." I'd never planned a birthday party, much less a whole wedding for two hundred people. I listened to Lana talk about what was going to happen, but as far as my contribution, I went to the tailor to get my tux fitted and I showed up. I also voted yes on having a wedding registry at Wally's Wine instead of a department store.

The ever-so-popular '80s mullet.
Thanks, Dad!

Mom, Dad, Jessica, and me, circa 1981.

My killer Michael Jackson impression at the fifth grade ice cream social.

My post-college modeling portfolio. Antonio Sabato, Jr. had nothing on me.

| HEIGHT: 5'11 | HAIR: Black | WAIST: 31 |
| WEIGHT: 175 | EYES: Brown | SUIT: 42/L |

The highway median wheat/sweater shot. Mom: "So handsome!" All of Hollywood: "*Zzzzzz.*"

SEBASTIAN

At the Four Seasons Beverly Hills in 1999. I was so relieved to get that job. At the time, I had no idea I'd still be working there six years later.

New Year's Eve at the Four Seasons, moments before leaving to do a set at the Comedy Store.

Introducing my sister Jessica, Mom, and Dad to Andrew Dice Clay, when I was opening for him in 2003.

Hanging out with my Chicago crew at my parents' house.

The Wild West Comedy Show comedians (left to right): me, Ahmed Ahmed, Bret Ernst, and John Caparulo, in 2005. Thirty days of nonstop laughter.

My first Showtime special (2012), *What's Wrong With People?* aka "What's Wrong With My Pants?" (PHOTO: DAN DION PHOTOGRAPHY)

The greatest weekend of my life in 2013 when Lana and I said, "We do."

(PHOTO: TORY WILLIAMS)

My second Showtime special (2014), *Aren't You Embarrassed?* My favorite special in terms of comedy. That magenta sweater drove me nuts!

Lana and me in 2014 at the American Comedy Awards in NYC. A couple hours later, I was in a headstand on the bed, hiccupping.

My third Showtime special (2016), *Why Would You Do That?* Filmed at the Beacon Theatre in NYC. Note the penguin shirt and matching Justin Timberlake shoes.

(PHOTO: TODD ROSENBERG)

At Patsy's in NYC with "Fucking Tony Danza" and a Frank Sinatra statue in 2016.

Proud parents.

(PHOTO: TODD ROSENBERG)

Lana loves to collaborate, and the wedding really took off when she met Marc Freidland, the guy who did our wedding invitations. Each invitation was a set of three boxes, each one designed and lined, one with gingham and fake grass, one with stripes, one with clouds. Inside each one was an invite to one of the separate wedding events: the rehearsal dinner, the wedding, and the wedding breakfast the day after. The overall wedding theme was "The Art of Love," and each event had a theme—"Our Love Is Surreal," "Isn't It Romantic?" "Take Love to the Streets"—and a symbol that was relevant to Lana. For example, the butterfly in the wedding invite box was about her father. At his funeral, they had released butterflies, and she associates them with him.

The location was a private home abutting a vineyard. The woman who owned it was a glamorous Italian socialite in her sixties, a big personality, a Sophia Loren type. She rarely (as in, almost never) rented out her grounds for events unless she liked you. So my wife went to meet this woman, and of course, she liked Lana. Everyone likes Lana. My wife admired photos of her and gushed about the French Provincial home, the cypress trees, and the pool. She and her husband were serious art collectors, and the yard was strewn with large sculptures, modern, very much to Lana's taste, too. Long story short, she agreed to let us have our wedding at her beautiful villa.

I knew a lot of our guests had to make the wedding their fall vacation because they had to pay for flights and hotels.

It was a lot to ask, and we were sensitive to that. I wanted my groomsmen—my five best friends from growing up and college—to stay in the same hotel as me, the Solage in Calistoga, so we could hang out all day by the pool.

The first night was an intimate dinner for just family at the Napa Valley Reserve, a private winery my father-in-law belongs to.

The rehearsal dinner was on the second night, a Friday, at the Solage. Lana and Marc figured out a way to project images on the walls of the space, like clouds and cartoon versions of our friends and family. After the meal, Lana and I sat on a lip-shaped couch and were the targets of a roast, MCed by my comedian friend Russell Peters. Four or five months before the wedding, I saw him at the Comedy Store and he said, "My gift to you is, I will DJ the wedding!" He does that on the side, but it could be his main gig he is so good.

"We're having a band," I said, "but if you want to DJ the rehearsal dinner and be the MC, that would be great." So he flew in on a private plane that day, and flew out after the party that night to make his gig in Vegas. He did it all on his own dime. That's a good friend.

Russell is like the Indian Don Rickles. His comedy is making fun of people, so he was the perfect guy for this event. There were drinks and amazing hors d'oeuvres, dancing, and then our closest friends roasted us and toasted us. My mom was hysterical. My sister killed. My dad's speech went over like a fart in church. For whatever reason, when he gets in front of people, he becomes a shell of himself. Lana's sisters went up. My friends raked me over the coals. John Petrelli told the story about our first date, and how Lana didn't talk (that got a lot of laughs). When the roast was over, unbeknownst to Lana and me, a wave of Vegas showgirl types had been hired to come out with those cigarette trays tied around their necks, but inside were copies of a mock *People* magazine, with Lana and me on the glossy cover. Inside were all the regular *People* columns and features and design, but all of it was about us and our lives. Every photo and article. The ads were about us, with our pictures. Even the crossword puzzle was about us.

The magazine was a labor of love by Lana's sister Heather. If the editors of *People* saw this, they'd hire her on the spot. Months before, she'd sent out a questionnaire to our guests asking for photos and ideas for this project, questions like "What's your favorite Sebastian moment?" When Heather is on any project, she is a woman possessed, but this was mind-blowing. She wrote it all, did the layouts, and had it printed so everyone could have a copy. This effort was above and beyond the call. There was so much love and so much enthusiasm for us from everyone there. It wasn't one of these superficial events where you invite people because they are so-and-so. Everyone there was a close friend or family, and they were being treated to this wonderful weekend.

The wedding was on Saturday. Alone, I put on my tuxedo

and did my hair. Then Eric Henning, my old friend and best man, and Rodney, Lana's brother, picked me up to drive to the estate. I remember that day being hot, so we gave out white parasols so people wouldn't bake in the sun.

The chuppah and chairs were set up in the backyard. Lana had designed the chuppah decorations of hanging bouquets and glass globes. Underneath it stood the rabbi and the priest. We are not very religious, but we wanted to have both of our religions represented, and we found these two men who work as a team.

While I watched the procession of flower girls and the wedding party and waited for Lana to come out in the dress I hadn't yet seen, but knew she'd spent three days in New York shopping for, I wasn't nervous at all. I felt only excitement and happiness. I could not wait to be married to her.

Finally, Lana appeared on the lawn in a dramatic white dress by Giambattista Valli. She looked like she was floating on a feathery cloud with a forty-foot-long train. I choked up as soon as I saw her, and was on the verge of crying for most of the ceremony.

We wrote our own vows. Mine were:

Being in Napa, I think it's fitting that a bottle of wine is much better when it's shared. I feel my life is so much better now that I get to share it with you. Lana, today in the presence of God and our closest family and friends, I want to tell you that I will forever be your one and only. I promise to be your clown when you need laughter. I promise to be your map when you need guidance. I promise never to make fun of Oprah. I will be your muse when you are searching for inspiration. I promise to be more accepting of people. And I promise to leave the thermostat at seventy-two degrees. Lana, I find something about you every day that makes me fall more madly in love with you. You have shown me what love feels like and for that I'm forever grateful. My heart will be your shelter and my arms will be your home. I love you, little one, and I can't wait to share the rest of my life with you.

I read them as best as I could while trying not to sob.

Lana went next. She kept a straight face when she delivered hers. She's much more in control of her emotions than I am. I happen to think it's because she's been through the worst of life with her father's sudden death when she was seventeen. Happy moments don't make her cry. She smiled reading hers. She made some of the same jokes about the thermostat and our different taste in TV shows, and "to remain calm when you wander off in the grocery store." But in the end, all that matters to me was her final line: "I'm so lucky to be on this journey with you while loving, learning, and walking together forever. I love you today and always."

The reception was jaw-dropping and started with a moment of drama and grace before anyone even had a chance to catch their breath after the ceremony. We'd hired ballerinas from a nearby ballet school to stand with big white balloons on strings among the cypress trees during the ceremony, and then they looped around to the reception area and took each balloon—with numbers on them—to the corresponding table to help people find their seats.

The band was outstanding. When they did a Beyoncé song, it sounded so perfect, I thought Bey herself was doing a guest spot. During our first dance—"Try Me" by James Brown— Lana paused, unhooked something, and stepped out of the long, fluffy part of the dress, revealing the top turned into a minidress that was underneath for dancing. I had no idea that puffy part came off. The creative surprises at this wedding just didn't quit.

My parents and in-laws made toasts during dinner. Again, my father fell flat. He said, "Let the good time rolls." That was his toast. He's Mr. Personality at his salon, but once he gets in front of a large group, forget it.

The food was incredible, not that I remember eating a single bite of it. The reception went by in a blur. There was so much going on, with the dancing and eating and drinking, talking to people and hosting. I remember this day, of the entire weekend, the least. I know I was overjoyed to be married, to share this experience with our guests, and that Lana's parents were paying for it. My parents did contribute, too. When the ballerinas appeared, Dad joked, "Did I pay for the dancers?"

The final event of the weekend was the Sunday brunch. My wife wanted to incorporate art into each event, so we set up a graffiti wall where people added their own painting and drawing on the overall wedding theme: "The Art of Love."

Our wedding was the greatest weekend of my life so far, by far. I'd never been a part of a huge production like that, the focus of so many people's brilliance and creativity. I was literally blown away. Our marriage has turned out to be a lot like our wedding: full of surprises and dramatic moments, popping with brilliance and beauty, and laughter all the way through.

7

SOUS CHEF

I've always taken pride in my style and thought of myself as a sharp dresser. BTW, Lana hates the word "sharp." She never used it growing up. I never found it strange until she told me it was, and then I asked around and others agree. I don't know if it's an Italian thing, generational, or Midwest speak, but whatever it is, I use it sparingly around her so I don't frost her bananas.

So the word "sharp" is out. Soon after Lana and I moved in together, I lost my confidence in my sharp dressing, too. I came home one day to find her and her friend Nazy in my closet, organizing and making a giveaway pile of some of my best clothes. Two of the most fashionable women I knew were trashing my wardrobe. My collection of Adidas tracksuits in every bright color? Gone. My Western plaid button-downs with an eagle embroidered on the front pocket? Trashed. They even put my Joop! cologne in the pile. I'd been looking for it for six months.

"Where'd you find this?" I asked, holding up the purple bottle.

Lana confessed, "I hid it a while ago."

"You don't like Joop!?" It had been my signature scent for years.

"Don't take it personally," she said, "but it gives me a head-ache. And a stomachache. And hives."

I gave it one last sniff and retired it into the cologne grave-yard.

I appreciated the brutal honesty, but the giveaway pile amounted to thousands of dollars' worth of clothes, not to mention the memories. Lana operated on a much higher taste level than I did. As an artist, her job was to have a sophisticated aesthetic. If she hated this stuff, I probably *should* get rid of it all.

My trust in my own fashion sense was completely rocked, and I turned over control of my look—head to toe, hair to shoes—to her. In fact, Lana was put in charge of all style-related purchases for us, including all of our clothes and home décor. I was relegated to handling the logistics, finances, electronics, travel, etc. This arrangement has worked well for us, and my style has improved exponentially. You can actually watch my four comedy specials to chart how my style has evolved—and improved—over the last ten years.

SEBASTIAN LIVE WAS filmed at the Pageant theater in St. Louis in 2007, but it got under way a couple of years before that. While I was on the Wild West Comedy tour, we stopped in St. Louis for a gig. After the show, the other guys and I were hanging out at a bar, and a man came up to me and said, "What are you doing here?"

It took a second, but I placed him as a longtime customer of mine at the Four Seasons in L.A. I remembered him because he was a great tipper. He'd just seen the show and was pleasantly surprised to find me in it. We got to talking, and he told me he worked for Budweiser, which happened to be one of the tour's sponsors. He was actually involved in the sponsorship program at the company, and he'd been sent to St. Louis to check out the tour. It was all such a small-world coincidence, we were both just shaking our heads.

"You know, Budweiser is thinking about launching a cable channel called Bud.TV. They want to get into the entertainment content business," he said. "Would you be interested in filming a special for us?"

"Absolutely," I said. It was the first time I'd ever been asked or approached about doing a comedy special on TV. I was flattered and excited by the prospect.

I got my agent and a lawyer involved, and the negotiations began. Initially, they wanted to shoot me at a comedy club, but they decided to do it in St. Louis (Budweiser's home base) at a big theater where the company could guarantee a packed house of their employees. They were going to give away free beer to draw a crowd, which was a good idea. There was no way I could bring in a thousand people on the strength of my name alone. At that point, I doubted I could draw eighty.

Ironically, Bud.TV hired the Levity Entertainment Group (LEG), which is now my management/production company, to shoot the special. It would be my introduction to the team and people I'd work with closely several years down the road, but for now, they were just the producers of this one show— hired guns.

In 2005, I was thirty-one years old, but still wet behind the ears as far as TV style was concerned. I wore a suit because I thought that was what you were supposed to do. In a suit, you were taken seriously. Problem was, I never had the right suit for the right occasion. This suit had a real traveling salesman look. It was black, and I paired it with a cerulean blue button-down shirt and cuff links. My foot was shoved into a dress shoe that was half the width of my extra-wide Fred Flintstone hooves. The jacket looked like what they would lend you at a hostess stand if you forgot yours. No tailoring. I got it on sale straight off the rack. I call it "sale to set," and it's not the effect you want for your first time on TV.

Bud.TV intended to chop up the hour-long special into four-minute clips, to use as connective tissue between their other programming. After one year, ownership of the material would revert back to me, and I could license the special to other networks and keep all the income I generated that way. It seemed like a great deal, and it kind of was.

I don't remember which came first, ownership of the special reverting to me, or Bud.TV shutting down. It only lasted a year, and then Budweiser got out of the entertainment business entirely. Now that I had the rights to the material, and by then a decent manager, we sold it to Comedy Central, a better home for it. In 2008, they aired it several times over the course of a year. Getting my name and face on a popular channel definitely increased my ticket sales, and my gigs got bigger and better.

There was no way Comedy Central would have produced the special for me, but since we had it ready to go, they were only too happy to put it on the air. If I hadn't met that Budweiser exec at the Four Seasons, and then run into him on the road, it never would have happened. The thing about comedy and success: You never know. When I served him his Budweisers in a frosted glass, I had no idea who he was, or what he would one day do for me. He liked me because I treated him well, and I remembered him because he was kind and generous. Random people you meet just might circle back into your life, and if you were an asshole the first time around, they won't be too happy to see you. And they definitely won't offer you a TV special.

FLASH FORWARD THREE years. By 2011, I'd officially signed up with LEG, and Judi Marmel was producing and managing the rollout of my second special, called *What's Wrong with People?* It was filmed in Santa Ana, California, in an old bank that was converted into a theater space with 450 seats.

Lana and I were a couple by then, and she had great ideas for the set design, the lighting, and the backdrop. We'd worked diligently and really thought through the set and the look of the show. We sent detailed notes to the design team. But when we got there, it turned out that they'd ignored most of our directions. We walked in, saw the set, looked at each other, and said, "Oh my God. Whose special is *that* going to be?"

The stage manger said, "Uh, yours."

Lana definitely doesn't seek out confrontation. But that day, she got so ruffled because this just wasn't our vision. They explained to us that they had had to add something to the front of the set for depth or it would have looked bad. Okay, then why didn't they run that by us? Also the lighting was all these crazy colors, a hodgepodge that made no sense to us and had to be fixed ASAP. That day was the first time Lana met my management team. I'd say, diplomatically, that the LEG people and Lana took careful measure of each other.

I preferred the set that Lana and I had chosen, but it wasn't as big a deal to me as it was to her. "It's about the standup," I said. "The audience doesn't give a fuck if the column lighting is gold or purple." However, as I would learn over ten years of doing these things, the audience might not realize they care about the aesthetics of the set, but the set represents me, and adds a vibe or a tone that affects their experience. The look does matter. It can make or break a performance. Lana has since become my creative director, handling everything from set design to wardrobe and promotional material. So if you like how the stage and the style of artwork on my tours look, you can thank her for it.

I was a bit overweight during that shoot. Despite the warm lighting, I came off as white and clammy, like the room was muggy and stifling. My outfit of tight black jeans, black shoes, brown belt, brown vest, and black shirt was dark, heavy, and unflattering.

"What were we thinking?" I asked Lana (and made a mental note to use that phrase as a possible title for a future special). We had picked out the outfit together, but I'd put on ten pounds since I bought it and the seams were hanging on for dear life. After seeing the playback, we both cringed.

It was a slipup. What you learn doing TV is that some clothes that look good on the hanger, or at a dinner table, aren't a good match for a standup comedy special. The worst part of the outfit was the jeans. People make fun of me to this day about how tight they were. I get comments like "nice camel toe." Even friends from home were like, "What the fuck, man?" This special was entitled *What's Wrong with People?* but they call it *What's Wrong with Your Pants?*

In terms of the comedy, I think it's one of my best specials. But when I look at it now, I'm distracted, just like the viewers probably were, by the style. I just don't look or feel my best. It didn't occur to me to hit the gym and get in shape as part of the preparation for shooting a TV special. I was more worried about getting the comedy right, rather than pumping up my abs.

I never want to fall into the trap of putting that kind of pressure on myself, and I don't beat myself up about things I can't change in the past. But, yeah, the style could have been better. A grade C outfit was not the end of the world. I'd do better next time. Because of the A+ comedy, there would be a next time.

I WAS IN great shape when we filmed the *Aren't You Embarrassed?* special in 2014. It was right around the time I got married, and Lana and I had been on a strict diet. We both had blood testing, and I learned I was allergic or highly sensitive to some of my favorite foods, like bread, pasta, and Scotch, and some random foods, like asparagus. For about six months, I cut all of them out of my diet, and I dropped twenty-two pounds.

I didn't change my diet to look good at the wedding. I'd been feeling low energy, sluggish. My wife hadn't been feeling so good either. She was so drained of energy she could hardly stay awake and focus. Turned out, she had a thyroid condition, an actual medical problem. My problem was that I was eating too much bread. The testing did inspire me to go on a health kick, watch what I ate, and work with a trainer again.

We shot in my hometown of Chicago, which should have guaranteed a good night. But I didn't particularly like that experience. I made the mistake of using a teleprompter for the first time. Sometimes, during a show, I'll forget to do a joke. When you film a special, you don't want to forget anything, because the jokes circle around and come together at the end. The teleprompter helped me remember the order and to hit every bit, but it also took me out of the moment and interrupted the flow. In just that second of looking down and then glancing up, you can lose the connection with the audience. I'm never as off-the-cuff shooting specials as I am at regular gigs.

We filmed two shows, back to back, with fresh audiences each time. The show that would air would be the better of the two, with maybe one or two bits spliced in from the other one. So I had to wear the same exact outfit for both performances.

For this show, I went with black jeans and a warm but thin magenta cotton pullover sweater. We were down to the wire choosing the look, and went with the magenta just moments before I walked out on stage. The sweater had one of these elastic bottoms, and every time I moved—and I move a lot in my act—the shirt would creep up and expose the skin of my belly and back. I was continually pulling the sweater back down over my belt. It was a constant but subtle tug-of-war throughout the filming.

My dad was at the taping, and he came back between shows and said, "Your shirt doesn't fit. I could tell from in the audience that you kept pulling it down." Nothing gets by this guy.

Wardrobe malfunctions are the worst, but I couldn't change now. We'd shot one of the two versions with the sweater, so I had to put on the clean identical one and wear it. It had to match, just in case we did some editing. I was pissed. "This stupid shirt keeps riding up and it's going to ruin the special," I said to everyone backstage. I liked the look of it, but it was taking me out of the moment. In the back of my head the whole time, I was worried that the shirt would be up to my tits while I was doing a joke. I did like how my hair looked in that one, though.

Speaking of hair, when Lana and I first met, my sideburns looked like a cross between Mr. T's and Elvis Presley's. Lana generously waited about a year before sending me to her hair guy. On top of the burns, my hairstyle was like a flattop petrified by copious amounts of hairspray and gel. If you bumped into my head, you'd have to get your outfit dry-cleaned. If my hair touched your face, you'd need a facial. Pre-Lana, I thought this look was sexy. Now I realize it was startling.

PRO STYLE TIP: For any event, from parties to weddings to comedy specials, do a dress rehearsal in an outfit before you commit to it.

WHY WOULD YOU *Do That?* was shot in 2016 at the Beacon Theatre in New York City. I did seven sold-out shows there and taped two of them. That was a crazy week. My father was there again. Mom stayed in California watching my nieces so my sister and brother-in-law could come, too.

The Chicago show was cool because it was my hometown, but the New York show was more of a grand event. It sounds cliché, but New York City really does have such incredible energy. I felt it from the crowd, and it fired me up. I think a lot of the people in New York gravitate toward my comedy because it's familiar to them. Many first-generation immigrants live in the city, lots of Italians. I get a great reception not just in Manhattan but on Long Island, in Brooklyn, down the shore in New Jersey. Anywhere in the Northeast is like I'm back in my own neighborhood.

Lana put the outfit together with a stylist friend named Michael Nash. Black pants, a white shirt with a black panel in front, like a penguin or a Kevlar vest. For the shoes, Michael said, "You might like these."

They were black-and-white, like spats. I loved them.

The stylist said, "I worked for Justin Timberlake on his 20/20 Tour, and Tom Ford designed these for him for the tour."

To be clear, these were not a copy of JT's Tom Ford shoes. These *were* the shoes that Justin actually wore on his own feet while singing and dancing (and probably sweating profusely) on his tour. He'd had twenty-odd pairs made. Michael had held on to two pairs that weren't trashed. They were my size, so he offered one pair to me.

I'm not the kind of guy who wears another man's shoes. But I did like the look, and they matched my shirt perfectly. So I searched high and low to find the same pair in retail, but it was impossible. You can't get them. They don't exist anywhere but with Michael and JT. So I bought Michael a pair of brand-new Tom Ford shoes, and traded them for Justin's hand-me-downs. As soon as I slipped them on, I felt like joining a boy band! They made me feel like dancing! And all week at the Beacon, I *was* especially agile on my feet.

I have a huge problem with sweating on stage. Always have, for my whole career. It's grossly evident whenever I perform in a light-colored shirt, something I learned early on not to do. A giant sweat ring does not look good on anyone.

I heard that if you get Botox injections in your armpits, you don't sweat as much. So I tried it. It works like a charm, but, as I say in my act, I think the sweat's rerouted itself and now my ass gets drenched every time!

When you're on stage, there is nowhere to hide. If you look at any physical performer—from Richard Pryor to Mick Jagger—these guys are soaked by the end of their shows, like they went through a carwash. For years, I've been on the hunt for a shirt that looks good and doesn't show sweat rings, and

I have finally found one. It's a polyester spandex blend from Uniqlo, black, with a sheen that makes it look wet already. If it gets soaked on stage, you can't tell. No rings in the pits. No blotches under the tits. I've worn it once already, in Biloxi, and it didn't creep up at all either.

PRO STYLE TIP: To hide sweat, go with polyester. It makes you sweat even more, but *no one will know.*

8

THE DRY SWALLOW

It was a big week, the biggest in my career so far. And in my sort-of-humble opinion, I was on top of my game.

Just to set the scene: November 2014, my second special for Showtime—*Aren't You Embarrassed?*—was coming out, and I was in New York to do a full week of press for it. I noticed a real shift in how this special was being received compared to my last one. In the almost two years since *What's Wrong with People?* came out, I'd been touring like an animal all over the world, working on my act, especially the physical side of it. I liked how my comedy was evolving, and this new special was the result of all that hard work. I was definitely feeling solid. I would never say "super confident," because I come from a family that always thinks negatively, but I was feeling really good.

Press week started on Monday with a radio tour. If you don't know what that is, you sit in a room with headphones and a microphone, and a producer patches you into a different station every five or ten minutes to do basically the same interview over and over again, like eighty times. It was a prolonged version of what Vince Vaughn did every morning on the Wild West Comedy tour. Like him, I knew how important it was to do the interviews, and I was happy to do them, but after three days straight of repeating myself, I was exhausted. I never slipped into autopilot, though. I kept up the energy, and even the sound guy gave me props.

So that was in the mornings. In the afternoons, my manager, agent, and I went to meetings—four a day—with editors and publishers to pitch this book. More talking, more pimping. It was the first time I'd ever pitched a book idea, and nearly every editor I met got a look on his or her face that said, "I just don't get this guy." I'd seen that look before, early on in my comedy career (one word: "sandman"), so it didn't affect me in the least. I went into every meeting with confidence that someone was going to get it and want to work with me. Most of the editors decided to "go in a different direction." I've heard this phrase a lot in my career. I always want to preempt it by asking before the meeting or audition, "What direction are you going in so I can follow the map on how to get there?" Some of the editors did like my story, and on the Friday of that week, we accepted an offer from Simon & Schuster. And just like that, a whole new avenue of my career opened up.

It was a week of riding high, of everything falling into place. I'd been working my ass off for fifteen years—no one could ever call me an overnight sensation—and it was all coming together for me, and so many people I cared about were there to share it. My mother, mother-in-law, wife, publicist, and management team were all there in New York with me, and I fed off their excitement, too.

The big week culminated Friday late afternoon with a five-minute set on Jimmy Fallon. It was my first time doing *The Tonight Show* with Jimmy Fallon, and the New York studio fascinated me. Right here, Johnny Carson had given so many comedy legends their start—Redd Foxx, Rodney Dangerfield, Bob Newhart, Don Rickles, George Carlin, Joan Rivers. Walking through the studio, I was looking at the wall of photos of previous guests, taking it in with awe that I was going to perform on the same stage.

For my Fallon *Tonight Show* premiere, I had to look sharp. Very important to me, always had been. When I was in high school, I didn't care about being a sports star or getting good grades. I just wanted to be voted Best Dressed (it's an Italian thing). I chose a three-piece dark blue Tom Ford suit with a crisp white shirt, no tie, and the watch my wife had given to me the day we got married. I was tan, with a fresh haircut and satin finish manicure. I felt like Frank Sinatra.

I brought everyone backstage with me, and entertained in the dressing room like I was hosting a small party, saying things like "You guys need any carrots, or anything like that?" I was in and out, chatting with people in the hall, making introductions, cracking jokes, and having a ball. I remember my mother-in-law walking around backstage talking to different people, from writers to producers. I think she even asked the stage manager if I could get some couch time with Jimmy.

A producer came to get me for a walk-through. I wasn't really paying attention as she led me around the stage—"Okay, the teleprompter is over there," she said. "You'll stand on this mark, you'll wait for Jimmy to join you after your set," etc.

In my head, I was thinking, *I've got my set down cold. I know what I'm going to do.* I generally don't like to look at a teleprompter because it takes me out of being in the moment, but I politely listened as she checked off her bullet points and did a sound check. Then I returned to my dressing room to wait for my cue.

My wife asked me how I was feeling, and I said, "Good." No nerves, no jitters. I'd had one hell of a week and couldn't wait to get out there and cap it off with an appearance on national TV.

Finally, they called me to the wings and Jimmy introduced me. Applause, applause, applause. I walked out on stage, looked to my right and gave Jimmy a nod, and got right into it.

Listen, so good to be here. I just ran into Liam [Hemsworth] backstage. That guy is stunning, all right? It's so good to be here. Jimmy Fallon. The Tonight Show. New York City. Love New York. A lot of Italians out here. I come from an Italian family, immigrant father. And if you come from immigrant parents, they put you to work real early. Okay? I've been working since I was eight years old. Watching TV, my father walks in the living room, he's like, "Hey, go start a business." Now?

The next bit should have rolled off my tongue, but nothing came out. I tried to remember what the next line was, but my brain was completely blank. I couldn't remember *anything*. I couldn't have told you my wife's name at that moment. I tried to prompt myself by saying, "I'm Italian . . ." but after that, nothing.

I was literally standing on that legendary stage, not saying a word, my eyes blinking, as shocked as anyone by the spectacle.

The entire place was completely silent. You could hear a pin drop in there—a grenade pin. I was bombing.

I turned to my left and looked at the band. Questlove was staring back at me with a look of fear in his eyes. They all were. I could almost hear them thinking, *This is the guy everyone's been talking about? He can't speak. He's literally losing it on* The Tonight Show.

So now, I remembered, *The prompter! Look at the prompter!* But I didn't know where it was because I hadn't paid attention during the walk-through. I scanned around for it, and finally found it, but by then, my eyes were blurry and I couldn't make out what the hell it said. I couldn't even read it. I remember thinking, *Do I need glasses? When the hell did my eyesight get so bad?*

It occurred to me that I had to start over from the beginning because this was worse than a midair collision. My five minutes were going by fast, and I had to snap out of this or they'd be completely gone. I started to look behind me to say to Jimmy, "I gotta start over," but as I turned my head, my brain rebooted, and my set popped back in.

So after that long, mortifying gap, I picked up where I had left off, saying, "They told me growing up, who had what I wanted in the neighborhood." My voice a bit subdued. The dead silence in the room was replaced with the audience's gasp of relief. *He can speak! Thank God.* I kept going.

They didn't buy us anything. We're like, "Dad, could we get a dog?" "You want a dog? Three houses down, they got dog. You want to pet something with fur, you walk three houses down, and then you come back here and cut my grass."

The audience started laughing. Maybe it was out of pity, but I didn't care. My mouth was forming the words and my body was moving. I was doing my set pretty well, but in the back of my mind, I kept thinking, *I'm fucked. I just shit the bed on national TV. I'm never coming back here again.*

It wasn't easy to be funny while mentally planning the funeral for my career. It was not the experience I'd hoped to have on that stage for the first time in front of two hundred people in the studio audience and 3.8 million at home.

I finished the set and Jimmy came on stage to announce a commercial break. I got to sit down with him for a minute and said, "Bro, I'm so sorry, I don't know what the hell happened to me out there. I'm just so sorry."

Jimmy said, "Don't worry about it. We can edit it out, no problem. It happens all the time." He was totally nonchalant about it.

"Oh, okay," I said, but my heart was hammering.

I went back to my dressing room and everyone congratulated me and told me how funny it was.

"How long?" I asked.

Lana said, "It was nothing."

"*How long?*"

"Thirteen seconds."

Thirteen seconds. For thirteen seconds, I stood up there, as frozen as a wedge of *tartufo*, while my family, managers, and every person in the theater watched in agony and I thought, *Did I just get fast-onset Alzheimer's disease?*

Think of how long thirteen seconds actually is. Right now,

count it out in your head. Time it on your watch. Imagine talking to a girl at a bar, entertaining her by saying, "You want to dance with me?" and then suddenly falling silent with your mouth flapping open for a full thirteen seconds while she stares at you, waiting for you to say something. By the time your brain rejoined reality, she'd be long gone.

I'VE RUN INTO trouble on stage before, falling out of my set and being unable to remember how to pick it back up. So that wasn't the first time I'd experienced a comedian's worst nightmare. But when you're on stage at a comedy club and you freeze, you can always just go to the audience. Pick out someone in the front row and say, "Where you from?"

It's a stalling technique, but it works. You take a minute to collect yourself, and a line or a bit will surface that you can grab onto like a life preserver.

Grasping in a vast blankness of the mind doesn't happen to me often—knocking wood, spitting in the evil eye—but there are triggers. If somebody in the first few rows starts looking at their phone, I immediately think, *They're not paying attention. They're not interested in what's going on up here.* I'm not so insecure and sensitive that I need every single audience member to be riveted by every jewel that drips out of my mouth, but when someone is scrolling through Instagram while I'm in the middle of a performance, it's a distraction. The phone light goes on. The person's face starts glowing. It's just as annoying to the people in the seats around them. I can't help but be knocked out of my act. So what I do is address the phone user, especially early on in the set. I understand people are going to look down for a second now and then. Maybe they got a babysitter and they're checking for emergency texts. I use a stock joke and say, "Hey, what are you looking . . . Is it the babysitter? Isn't the reason you got a babysitter . . . Are you babysitting them?" And then I go, "When I grew up, my parents left the house, they didn't come back for three days."

It's a way to address the problem, let them know I don't like it, and keep the show rolling. If I have to call someone out, I do it in a nice way (unless someone is not nice back, then the gloves come off). The audience is there to relax and have a good time. If you come back at someone hard, the audience tightens up. They feel like they have to behave and be proper—the opposite vibe from what you want in a comedy club.

When you're taping for TV and get stuck, however, you can't go to the audience. You can't even go to the camera guy and say, "Nice shirt. Did your mom pick that out for you?" The camera—which is so big, a guy rides in it—is right in front of you, and the audience is a mile away, it seems, and obscured by lights. Plus, the format of TV taping is pretty rigid. You hit your mark, do your set, and if there's time and the host likes you, you sit on the couch and banter for a minute. In fact, most likely, your five-minute set is preapproved. You have to write it out word for word and hand it in. They make it very clear that you're not supposed to stray from the material you said you were going to do.

Before what is known in my house as "The Night I Shit the Bed on Fallon" (as in, "Hey, babe, what hotel were we staying at 'The Night I Shit the Bed on Fallon'?" "The London." "Right, thanks"), I'd done plenty of TV. I knew exactly what to expect and what I had to do. But my years of experience evaporated during those thirteen seconds. It was like I was twenty-five again, back at Highland Grounds.

Comedians work their whole lives for a shot on *The Tonight Show*. In the early days of standup, it was *the* venue, the one place that could launch a career into the stratosphere. Nowadays, comedians have more options, but there's still a reverence associated with this stage. Only the best of the best get there. The stakes were sky high for me to kill, and I blew it.

I honestly thought my career was over, that those thirteen seconds would be the number one viral video on YouTube the next day. "Comedian Shits the Bed, Whole House on Fallon." "Comedian Literally Dies Up There on *The Tonight Show*." "Comedian Keeps Repeating 'I'm Italian' on Fallon. Duh, We Know!"

You might say I was overreacting. You don't think thirteen seconds of horrible could destroy a decades-long career?

Look, I was sinking in quicksand for thirteen seconds, convinced I was going to drown. If I'd had the power of perspective, I would have told myself, *Sebastian, you're going to be okay. You'll laugh it off, and it'll be fine.* During the interminable silent gap, though, for the rest of the set and the remainder of the evening, all I could think was *It's over. I am fucked. Thank God my father isn't here.*

AFTER THE TAPING, we went to Osteria Morini on Lafayette Street in Soho, a Northern Italian–style restaurant recommended by my manager Chris Mazzilli, a man who can name and rate a hundred Italian restaurants in New York off the top of his head. I'd been looking forward to this meal, and had spent an hour on the website, poring over the menu, drooling. The dinner was supposed to be the cherry on top, the big celebration of my week of triumphs—the special, the tour, the book deal. And Fallon.

I was a wreck. I sat down at the table. It was a nice place, rustic with long farm tables. I would love to go back there under more pleasant circumstances, but it was all I could do not to get up and leave the restaurant. I'm emotional, a crier, a man who lets it all out in front of other people, quivering chin, ugly cry face. I love to marinate in my own tears. I held them in at that dinner, mainly because I was still in shock.

Everyone was talking about what to order, the handmade *tagliatelli* with Bolognese ragú; the *cappelletti* with truffles, ricotta, and prosciutto; the rack of lamb with arugula-anchovy pesto; the forty-day aged tomahawk rib eye. I'm getting hungry typing the menu now, but at the time, my appetite was gone.

"Do you think it was okay?" I kept asking. "It's going to look like shit, probably."

Lana said, "Just forget about it. It's over. We're at this amazing restaurant. Have some mortadella and relax. There is nothing you can do."

For the first time in my life, mortadella did not make me happy.

"Eat, Sebastian," said my ma.

"I'm not hungry," I said.

The whole table stopped and looked at me. For me to refuse food, this was serious. My mom probably thought about calling 911. I'm always *starving* after a performance, but at Osteria Morini, I couldn't eat one bite. I tried to rally my spirits, but how could I enjoy myself? I didn't know what the edit was going to look like when it aired later that evening. I couldn't relax until I saw it. Were 3.8 million people going to point at their screens and say, "Look at the idiot!" It was too much to contemplate, yet I couldn't stop thinking about it.

My family and friends reassured me at dinner. They described their reactions to my brain freeze while they watched it live in the green room.

My wife said, "We all looked blankly at one another, holding our breath, more tongue-tied than you."

My manager Chris, owner of the Gotham Comedy Club,

has seen hundreds bomb on stage. He said, "I kept saying, 'Oh my God, oh my God,' over and over. So, yeah. It was bad."

My mother-in-law said, "Your suit looked beautiful."

Mom said, "I've just never seen you like that before. It was . . . suspenseful?"

They were trying to crack me up, and I pretended to go along with it. I choked down some pasta, but every bite was a dry swallow.

Lana and I went back to our hotel room at the London. It was already turned down, and I love turn-down service. There is something about leaving your room a mess and coming back at the end of the night with a treat on your pillow and a bottle of water on the nightstand. It's always an added bonus when they leave a card with the temperature for the following day. This was the first time the turn-down service didn't make me happy. I was too anxious to lie down. I had to see the Frankenstein hack job of my set before I could hope to relax.

Lana was having none of it. She kept insisting it would be fine, but how could she know? We had to wait and see.

Finally, at 11:30 p.m., five hours since the taping, the show started. I barely heard Fallon's intro. Liam Hemsworth came on, and Lana said, "He really is stunning."

"I know, right?"

And then it was my turn. I got through the first forty-five seconds of my act with confidence and swagger. There was a quick cutaway to a different camera angle that picked me up as soon as my brain started working again. If you check out the video on YouTube (viewed 1.6M times; 1.5M by me), right at :46 seconds, it looks like I'm coming out of a coma. My voice is shaky; my eyes look dazed, or haunted. But I did recover, and after a rocky five or ten seconds, I got back into the rhythm of my set and made it through.

Jimmy joined me on stage to shake my hand, all smiles and upbeat. I looked hollowed out. I gave him a traumatized glance, but he started jumping around, mimicking my moves and I followed suit. He did exactly the right thing to bring the energy up. Easy for him. He knew my gap would be edited out, but I didn't.

I turned to Lana and said, "Not a disaster."

"Not even close," she said, smiling. "Are you okay now?"

"Actually, to tell you the truth, I'm starving."

Now that the hundred-pound anvil of dread was gone, my stomach was desperately empty.

I ordered the branzino. When room service brought it up, the guy looked at me and said, "Be careful. There may still be a few bones. I don't want you to choke!"

I said, "Great, I already choked once tonight."

WE LIVE IN a world where everybody is always talking about how fantastic his or her life is. Vacation photos, toasting on a boat with champagne, celebrations and achievements. That's what people put on social media. Everyone is just bragging all the time, or humble bragging, which is even worse. It's like nobody ever fucks up or does anything wrong.

But people do fuck up in life, all the time. We make mistakes, big and small. We all have stories to tell about the not-so-good times, and I happen to believe those are the ones we should share. It would be like a public service so everyone doesn't think being perfect is the norm.

If you pretend nothing's wrong, then you don't take the step of asking, "What the hell happened?" Since my career and my family's security relies on me *not* shitting the bed/whole house/entire neighborhood on TV, I needed to know what had caused my brain to betray me that night, and take measures so that it never occurred again.

I think what happened was a deadly combo of overload and overconfidence.

The overload was all the craziness that week. There was so much going on. I was talking, talking, talking on the radio tours; I was pitching the book. I was doing other interviews about the special. I had people in town and felt responsible for entertaining them. My head was spinning in a bunch of directions, and by the time I stepped onto that stage, it had spun clear off my neck.

The overconfidence was thinking I could handle doing everything at once, no problem. I thought I could just go up there and do standup as if it were no big deal. It was like saying a smug "I got this" while falling off a bridge. I didn't respect the mental demands of doing a live comedy set on national TV. It was almost like, after a week of glutting my ego with positive feedback, I forgot the philosophy of life that had gotten me this far: Stay Hungry. Pare it down. Keep focused on what you're doing and on the reasons you're doing it.

I would never again be too casual about any performance, anywhere. Since Fallon, I reset my pre-show routine. If I have people in the dressing room, I kick them out ten minutes before I go on stage. Or they can sit there in stone silence while I review video of previous gigs and collect my thoughts. I get in my own space rather than inviting others into it. Afterward, we can talk and laugh and (most likely) eat. But before I go on, no talk, no food, clear head, no distractions.

ONE MONTH AFTER the Fallon disaster, I did Conan.

Back on the horse that bit me on the ass.

I kept thinking about the yips, a phenomenon when a pitcher suddenly can't control the ball. He's throwing it, doing his regular motion, and the ball goes wild. No matter how he adjusts, he can't fix it. It's totally mental.

I got it in my head that the yips could happen to me. I thought, *Shit, will I freeze every time I go on TV? Is this going to be the new awful normal?*

To ward off the yips, I took the concept of staying hungry to the extreme. It was like I was training for a marathon. The whole week leading up into Conan, I ran my set in the bathroom. I ran it in the shower. I ran it with my wife.

The day of the taping, I had Lana and one of my managers with me. You better believe I paid attention to the walkthrough that time. I could do a full to-scale rendering of the stage—and the teleprompter location—from memory that day.

Complete change of wardrobe. I wore a thin black cashmere sweater and black jeans, black shoes. Television studios are kept icy cold, and it was December. Still, I was sweating. We were in the dressing room and it was getting close. I told my wife, "Get out. I gotta be alone." She got up to leave. I said, "Get back in here and let me do the set in front of you." She came back in. I said, "No, leave." I was driving her nuts.

And then the moment of truth. I was called to the stage and began.

I'm dealing with a possum problem at the house. Just moved into a new house. Me and my wife like to go in the yard at night, have a little wine. And these possums are comfortable, *like if they could talk, they'd be like, "What the hell are* you *doing here?" Now, I grew up in an immigrant family, and how we handled possums, raccoons, my father would be like, "We're going to murder the bastards. We're going to pour antifreeze on bologna." What?*

That was the forty-five-second mark, the point on Fallon when it all went to hell. On the video of this performance, my eyes are clear. I am totally present and in the moment. I look up with a huge smile on my face because I remembered *everything*. The next line was right there, and I punched it.

I woke up in the morning, birds, squirrels, raccoons, just murdered all over our property. Neighbors coming by. "Have you seen our cat?" "No, we haven't seen it. Check the yard."

I killed on Conan, and I proved to myself that I wasn't cursed with the yips. I'd redeemed myself and gained perspective on what could happen when you get too comfortable, too confident.

Redemption is a theme in my life, the drive to correct mistakes and rectify wrongs. Lana knew what it meant to me to walk off Conan's stage in one piece, and she gave me a big hug in the dressing room. No tears. By the end of the night, my face hurt from smiling so hard.

She said, "How do you feel now?" My wife is like a shrink, always asking how I feel.

"*Hungry*," I said. "Where you wanna eat?"

9

ICING ON THE CAKE

The American Comedy Awards are the most important awards that you have never heard of—at least to us comedians. I wouldn't call them the Oscars or Emmys of comedy, though. The Oscars do (rarely) award prizes to comedic films, and the Emmys give a nice showcase for funny TV shows and performers. But the Lucys, as the ACA statue was called, after Lucille Ball, were a very big deal (especially for the winners).

When I was nominated in 2014 for Best Club Comic, I was in shock. The other nominees—Maria Bamford, Bill Burr (my old neighbor), Jerrod Carmichael, Ron Funches, Kyle Kinane, Sean Patton, Brian Regan, Rory Scovel, and Doug Stanhope—are all top-tier people I admire, especially Brian Regan.

My introduction to Brian's comedy was in 1988, at a

Thanksgiving dinner, watching him on TV. He had a bit about getting a snow cone after a Little League baseball game. The way he told the story, his distinctive delivery and how he acted it out, is what made it so funny. It can't be translated into words (Google "Brian Regan Little League"). Brian's ability to convey his message through his body and vocal inflections adds dimension to his comedy. In 2016, I got to see it up close while working with him at the Oddball Comedy Festival. His is the type of act you can see over and over. You laugh just as hard the tenth time you hear the material as you did the first time. He's the type of comedian other comedians backstage gather around the monitors to watch. I've heard he takes a shot of peach schnapps—the too-sweet pink liquor in Sex on the Beach, the Bikini Martini, and the Fuzzy Navel—before every show. On the Oddball tour, I joined him in this ritual for shits and giggles.

All of the other nominees in my category were entrenched in the comedy world. I was never really a member of that club, nor had ever participated in any popularity contests. I'd always kept an eye on who got nominated for such awards, though, and wondered who the hell was in charge of choosing the list.

When I heard the news, I called my managers, figuring there was some sort of mistake, but they confirmed the nomination was real. I was up for a Lucy and I was invited to the award ceremony at the Hammerstein Ballroom in New York a few weeks later. The event organizers weren't providing air travel or hotel reservations, but they were serving a barely edible meal and free drinks.

If I didn't attend and I actually won, the presenter would have to say, "Sebastian Maniscalco isn't here tonight because he tried on his wedding tuxedo, couldn't button it, and didn't have time to get the waist let out. I will accept this award for him."

On the off chance the presenter was going to say my name, I wanted to be there to hear it. Did I feel a need to be in the room, to look pleasantly surprised, kiss my wife, stand up, pretend to trip dashingly as I wove my way through the maze of tables to accept my award, and deliver a speech that would be a bonanza of laughter and tears? No. I never did comedy for awards. But it is nice to be recognized, to get a kind of milestone marker in your career. I think all performers have fantasized about what they would say at the podium. If for nothing else than because it would be nice to thank those who helped me along the way.

First order of business: my outfit. Since NBC was televising the awards in prime time (another reason to be there), I decided on my Tom Ford wedding tux. True to form, it didn't fit anymore. Last time I'd worn those pants was around two years prior, and I had been sixteen pounds lighter. When I managed to close them, the button and buttonhole were hanging on to one another for dear life. If I wore them like that, they might have left a permanent line on my belly like I'd had a C-section. I tried buttoning the jacket and wearing a vest, but who was I kidding? The muffin top at this point was more like a popover. I wore the tux anyway. Even tight, it was my best option.

I wrote an acceptance speech. I practiced it in our hotel room at the London the night of the award show. Lana was taking forever to get ready. It was a special night, so I didn't want to rush her and get into an argument. I took a deep breath in an attempt to find my friendly voice and asked, "Babe, you almost ready?"

"One second!" she replied from the bathroom.

Twenty minutes later, she emerged. She was worth the wait. She looked stunning in a tangerine Dior dress with spaghetti straps and a peek of pink lining at the handkerchief hem.

"Do you like these earrings, or the other ones?" she asked.

Any answer I gave her would be the one that got us out the door faster, hence, "The ones you have on are perfect."

We hopped into an Uber just as a downpour started. On the way, I asked Lana to close my shirt buttons. I didn't ask her earlier because it would have taken up even more time. So she went to do them, but there was a problem. They weren't going in the holes. I'd never seen this type of button before. You needed an engineering degree to figure them out, and I had only a corporate organizational communications degree. I was sweating, digging my chin into my collarbone to see, and twisting my torso like I was in Cirque du Soleil. Lana tried to get them in while I sucked in my popover to make sure the pants button didn't fly off and shatter a window. In a fit of frustration, I called my guy Jason at Tom Ford (Lana had the number) and said, "Man, my shirt is screwed up! I can't get the fucking buttons in."

He walked us through it, and we finally got them in. But by now, I was flustered and my neck was drenched. It wasn't a great start to what could be a significant evening for my career.

The driver got us as close as he could to the entrance—I think he dumped us at the bus stop on the corner—and we got out. I opened my umbrella and we walked up to the security guards. Before we could explain things, they directed us toward the general admissions line to get into the ballroom.

"I'm supposed to walk the red carpet. I'm nominated," I informed them.

"You?" one said.

"Yeah."

"Really?"

After a moment of hesitation, they pointed us toward a check-in tent across a rainy path full of puddles. We trekked through the weather to the tent and went up to the woman who appeared to be in charge. She said, "Hi, there. The general admissions entrance is that way."

"I'm nominated," I said, starting to feel like an idiot. I don't like to sound arrogant or brag or say, "Do you know who I am?" But in this case, I had to say something or I'd never get into the room.

She shot me the same look of disbelief as the security guys.

They had to go through a binder that looked like a yearbook and search through the photos to try to find my face. Even after they found it, they still questioned me as if I were trying to fraudulently enter the red carpet. It was like there was no way possible I was meant to be there. I felt like Julia Roberts in *Pretty Woman*, but finally, they confirmed that I had the same huge forehead as the guy in their book.

As soon as we hit the red carpet, we were blinded by a flash of lightning. Not real lightning. A hundred camera flashes had gone off because Seth Rogen was in front of us, standing in front of the "step and repeat" wall with the American Comedy Awards logo on it. Seth negotiated that scene like a pro. He was smiling and at ease, a natural.

Next, it was our turn. Lana said, "You go. I'll meet you at the end."

"No way," I said. "You're coming with me."

If you know anything about my wife, she goes with the flow. If I wanted her to try something, she was game. If I want to do something on my own, she's cool with that, too. That night, I wanted her with me. So we walked together. As we began, the PR rep announced my name, which apparently was a cue for the photographers to clean their lenses. I waited for them to be done and told myself, *They must really want clean, crisp photos of me.* I walked along the carpet, twisting and turning, with no flashes going off, feeling a little conspicuous and uncomfortable. And then finally, a photographer called my name. "Sebastian! Sebastian! Move aside. I want one of Lana by herself."

What, for his private collection?

I stepped aside and the lightning storm went off for my wife. This went on for the rest of our red carpet walk, people yelling at me to get out of the way. I was a good sport, laughing along.

We entered the ballroom and found our seats at a table for eight in the middle of the room. Once we were seated, I shook off my annoyance and remembered why we'd made the trip. It was exciting to be in the room. Chris Rock was there to present a lifetime achievement award to Bill Cosby (pre–rape allegations). A quick glance around, and I saw Kate McKinnon, Amy Poehler, tons of comedy all-stars. We settled in and Lana had a cocktail. I was holding off because I wanted to be clearheaded for my award.

As I continued to gawk around at the other nominees, I realized something that made my heart sink. I said to Lana, "Nobody is here from my category except Maria Bamford."

As the dinner was served and the show got started, I checked the program to see how many nominees from other categories had shown up. "Nine people up for Best Concert Comic, and only Jim Gaffigan is here," I said to Lana. I was making a study of this, hoping it didn't mean what I feared it did.

As the awards were announced and people started going up to receive them, I got the feeling that their joyful surprise reactions were fake. Some of them went up to accept *with props*. Seth Rogen and Evan Goldberg won for Best Comedy Director in Film for *This Is the End*. Seth said, "We first learned about the ACAs four days ago, and we came to receive the award in person because it's being televised and we were literally guaranteed to win."

Rogen and Goldberg knew they were going to win. They all *knew they were going to win.* Maria Bamford, I noticed, looked very relaxed, not on the edge of her seat at all, about our upcoming category. So if someone told her who the winner was, and no one told me, that could only mean that she was going to take home that award.

How did she know? I had to assume the ACA told her manager to make sure she'd show up. If the winning managers knew, did the losers' managers know, too? None of the other losing nominees were there. They had to know they hadn't won. *Why didn't my managers tell me?* As I was putting the puzzle pieces together, I felt like Jim Carrey in *The Truman Show*. Everyone else knew what was going on. I was the only asshole who didn't.

And I was hungry, too. I hadn't eaten the food because I thought I might give a speech and I didn't want roasted baby carrots stuck in my teeth. You know the self-control it takes for me to pass up dinner, even a gross piece of rubber chicken!? A fucking lot. What a putz I was, sitting there.

The joke was on me. I had written my speech. I'd practiced it. When my category was announced, the cameraman zoomed in on me, tight. That moment was funnier than anything else. I'd just figured out what was going on, and I had to pretend like I was still hoping. My "people to thank" card was poking out of my pocket. I had to wonder if the camera guy was in on it, too, and the producers in the truck outside. Were they saying into the cameraman's earpiece, "Get in close on Sebastian. Holy shit! He wrote a speech! He doesn't even know he's going to lose! He actually thinks he's got a shot! Zoom in on the index card!"

The presenter announced Maria Bamford's win. I was thinking, *Whatever happens, clap and smile and act like you're happy for her.* Even if I hadn't figured out I'd already lost, I would have felt the sting of disappointment. It wasn't a crushing blow. It would have been nice to win, but, as always, I was just glad to be there.

I applauded. I listened to her short speech thanking a list of people. My speech had an arc, a climax, a plot, main characters, and finished with a denouement. It was so good, they would have given me an award next year for Best Acceptance Speech.

Now that I knew for absolutely sure I would not have to do or say anything, I started to let loose and began drinking Bacardi and Diets. The Hammerstein Ballroom staff might have been in on the fix, because they kept bringing me more drinks. Sometime between numbers three and four, I got the hiccups.

When Bill Cosby got his lifetime achievement award, he

gave the longest acceptance speech I have ever heard in my entire life. It was like your grandpa telling you old war stories. It was so quiet in the room, I was trying to hold back hiccups, but about every thirty-two seconds, one would come up and there was nothing I could do to stop it. My wife was looking at me in disbelief. She knew that when I get the hiccups, they last for hours. We were seated right in camera view, so we couldn't get up and leave in the middle of Cosby's endless talk. I was desperate to make the hiccups stop, but I couldn't do anything about it.

Cosby finally stopped talking, and a lot of the comedians in the crowd went up on stage to join him in his celebration. Not me. I'm not good at the end of anything—dancing, clapping, waving to the crowd, hugging people, or searching for someone's hand to shake. What were they talking about up there? I had no idea. Instead, Lana and I slipped out.

When the show was over, Lana said, "What now?"

Take a wild guess. I was *starving*. "Let's go out to dinner."

"Where?"

A week earlier, I'd tried to get us a reservation at Carbone on Thompson Street, the hardest restaurant to get into in NYC. The woman on the phone told me in what I call a "nice mean" voice that the place was completely booked for the next four calendar years.

I looked at Lana in her gorgeous dress, I looked down at the buttons we put so much sweat into fastening on me. We *had* to salvage this night. I hiccupped again and said, "Fuck it, we're going to Carbone."

Lana said, "Even though we couldn't get a—"

"I don't care. Let's go."

GROWING UP, I went out to dinner with my parents and grandparents as often as the World Cup: once every four years. We would go to the same place every time, Gianotti's. It was the only time I ever saw my grandmother out of her salmon-colored nightgown. You knew it was a special night whenever my father did his mother's hair in the makeshift salon he had set up in the basement, followed by my mother and then my sister. My dad hated this. He had already worked sixty hours that week, and these three women were the most difficult clients he had. They didn't pay and they tried to micromanage him. When they told him what to do, he would say, "Nobody told Michelangelo how to paint the Sistine Chapel. Now, *ba fa goule.*"

At Gianotti's, we would start right in discussing what we were thinking of having. Then my dad would announce what he was going to order, which signified that we could get anything on the menu equal to or less than what he chose. If you wanted a steak and he was thinking pasta, too bad! There was always next time, in just four short years.

God forbid you left anything on your plate. You would get

a lecture from my father about wasting food and (his) money, while he polished off one unfinished plate after the next. He ate like a Viking, littering bones and shells all around him. Watching him, you might cringe, but you couldn't look away. The man could gnaw on a lamb chop while deboning a fish.

Toward the end of the meal, an uncomfortable anticipation always came over the table because the kids were going to want dessert—chocolate cake, key lime pie, cheesecake. However, my grandmother had invariably just made seventeen different types of cookies—*giuggiulena, cucidati, biscotti*—that all tasted the same: dry. We ordered dessert at Gianotti's maybe once ever, and my grandmother was so insulted, she sulked for a week.

There was always a struggle between my grandfather and my father over the bill. My father would do everything he could to prevent my grandfather from seeing the total cost. If he did, he'd fly into a Sicilian rage cursing in rapid-fire Italian. I would ask my father, "What did he say?" The answer was always, "There are no words in English." I knew it had something to do with how my grandmother could have made a better meal for a fraction of the price that would have fed the whole neighborhood for two weeks.

At Gianotti's, I was introduced to the Salvatore Maniscalco banking system. He would pull out of his pocket a worn envelope. It was covered with water damage and coffee stains and had possibly been passed down from out of my great-grandfather's pocket. I would ask, "Dad what *is* that!?" In a panel in the ceiling, he hid several envelopes that were stuffed with cash. One was for "going out." Others were marked "landscapings," "fix," and "rainy days." To pay the restaurant tab, he would take bills out of the envelope, line them up perfectly with all the presidents' heads facing in the same direction. Until the waiter came to take the money, Dad would count and recount it, and tap the pile of bills like he was burping a baby. During this whole time, you could not talk to him. He was staring at the wall, thinking about how many perms and dye jobs he would have to do to replenish the envelope.

My father is a 20 percent tipper across the board when we go anywhere. As a hairstylist, he earns his living off tips, so he is very mindful of others in the service industry. When he goes out with people, he gets nervous that when the bill is split, they won't tip as well as he does and that he'll be guilty by association.

SALVO'S PRO TIPS ON TIPPING

1. Cash is king! Always have a knot of cash to cover the cost of the meal and tip in cash.

2. Carry several bills in each denomination. Be prepared to pay the bill in exact change so the waiter doesn't have to bring anything back. Round up to the nearest dollar amount.

3. Always hand the waiter the tip. You want your face to be associated with the cash. Do not just leave the tip on the table. If you walk out that door, someone else may pocket it.

LANA AND I took a taxi to the West Village and walked into Carbone without a reservation. I might not have won the Lucy, but I was determined to redeem myself by getting a table. I know there are hundreds of excellent restaurants in New York City, but it was a point of pride for me to get into this one. I had supreme faith that we would. It was the power of the tux. If you're dressed up, you have a little bit more confidence. If we had been in jeans and T-shirts, forget it. But we were in black tie. *Good* black tie.

We entered the dark restaurant with sexy, low lighting and walked right up to the hostess stand. Why do hostesses always have an attitude as if you're interrupting them? They glare at you when you walk in, like, "Oh, you think I'm actually gonna take you to a table here? Who do you think you are?" Even when you say, "Yes I have a reservation," they question it, or they seem to hope they won't find your name on the list, or they act as if they'd get pleasure telling you to take off. If they make any negative grunts at all, I scan the list and find my own name upside down. You know how hard it is to read "Maniscalco" upside down? Most people can't even read it right side up.

The Carbone hostess was a piece of work right off the bat, but I wasn't going to let her get to me. Not in the tux. The tux doesn't take bullshit. The tux won't be denied. I said, "Good evening," in my sweet, friendly, I-have-a-tear-soaked-acceptance-speech-in-my-pocket voice. It was the voice of a guy you would want to pull a few strings for. I spoke quickly, though, because I had to fit all this in between hiccups. I tried to throw in a quick comedy bit, but it bombed. When people ask me who the toughest audience is, I tell them, "Any girl in her early twenties working as a hostess at a hot restaurant in New York."

She fake smiled and said, "How may I help you?"

"Do you happen to have anything for two?"

"For *tonight*?"

"For right now."

She gave a little laugh that signified, "I'm in control, and you're out of luck." But before she shot me down, I reached into my pocket to take out a hundred-dollar bill. I said, "We don't have a reservation but we're starving. It's our only night in the city and we heard we have to come here."

"It's impossible."

Then I slipped the hundge into her hand and said, "Let me know if anything suddenly opens up." The bill was snatched out of my hand the way a hungry alligator snaps up prey and then softly sinks into the water. It disappeared so fast into her pocket, I thought for a second that I hadn't given it to her at all.

Fifteen seconds later, a guy in a black suit escorted us to a table. It was the best table in the house, hugging the window and giving us an unobstructed view of Thompson Street. It was like the Copa scene from *Goodfellas*. I don't know if they brought a table up from the basement, but suddenly, we were seated.

I have been on the other side of the hundge slip, and it worked on me, too. At the Four Seasons, a guy gave me $100 to move somebody out of a specific table (secluded, outside) so he could sit there. He put the bill in my hand and said, "See what you can do." I marched right over to the table and told the women there, "A large party is coming in and they had a reserve on this table. Would you mind moving? Next round is on me." They moved and I spent $30 on their drinks, but I walked away with $70, and it made my night. I would have done a lot more for less. A hundred-dollar bill makes you *move*. There's something about it. You don't see it often, it's like an eclipse. It's the most you can give somebody in a single bill.

In NYC, they get it. A hundred has influence. It means something. You give one to the right person, boom, you're set.

In L.A., with the exception of myself at the Windows

Lounge, the servers are clueless. They don't get it at all. My wife and I went to a restaurant called Felix, a hot spot in Venice. It's practically impossible to get in, but I called my agent, who is tapped into the food world, and he got us a reservation for Lana's birthday. We had wine, a variety of pastas, some dessert. No bill, because my managers picked it up for us as a gift. I still gave the waiter a tip, though. He was going to get 20 percent regardless, but I gave him a crisp hundge, and said, "Thanks for a great meal. Let me ask, who's the guy we need to talk to next time we want to come back?" In other words, "This is not a tip. It's a payoff for a connection."

He said, "Oh, wow! Thank you. So next time you want to come in, you can call the reservation desk during the day, during business hours."

I said, "No, who's *the guy*? The guy I need to talk to in order to make sure we get in."

"Well, what a lot of people do is come down here and wait to see if anyone canceled their reservation." He was looking at me cross-eyed the whole time.

With patience, I said, "Who's *the guy*!"

Lana said, "Don't bother."

So at Felix, I tried to pull a Dice-style Pro Deal move, to no avail.

Back in New York, at Carbone, I was in. When you tip a hundred, word travels faster than the speed of sound through the back of the restaurant, and we were inundated with service. The water guy showed off his pouring technique like a human Bellagio fountain. The bread guy was juggling loaves, carving our portraits into the cold butter. The sommelier was out within seven seconds from wherever he goes when he isn't helping to pick out a bottle. Do they keep him in a closet where he can groom his nose with artisanal tweezers while wearing a tongue mask giving his taste buds a facial? Usually, it takes a sommelier a while to get to the table, like he's tied up on an emergency phone call. That night, he was all over us.

Once you tip a hundred bucks at the door, you can't just order one soup and split it. We had to live up to the tip, and that meant appetizers, entrées, desserts. Lana tells me that we had a fantastic, unforgettable meal, along with a fantastic bottle of wine. On top of the four cocktails I'd had, the wine put me way over the top, so I have no recollection up until the tiramisu, which jolted me awake like smelling salts.

Meanwhile, my hiccups never went away. If anything, they had only gotten worse. Back at the hotel room and blissfully out of my excruciatingly tight pants, we tried to cure me of them. Lana was Googling and reporting all these folk remedies—drinking water while pinching your nose, breathing into a white paper bag, holding your breath while doing neck rolls. I did everything I possibly could to get rid of them. Nothing worked. So I came up with my own solution of doing a headstand on the bed. I put my head on the mattress and kicked my feet in the air like a frog for thirty minutes. Apparently, when you go into shock and all of the blood in your body goes to your amygdala, the hiccups disappear.

PRO TIPS FOR TRAVEL TIPPING

These days, I travel twenty-eight weekends a year, and I've got my travel tipping routine down. As a general rule of thumb, you grease good people who can get you stuff. That's how it works in hospitality. I take care of you, you take care of me. I give a lot of tips. You do what you want to do, but this is how I do it, as a guy who is constantly on the road and in the air.

- **The driver.** For the drivers to and from the airport, generally the tip is included in the fare that you pay ahead of time by card. You don't have to tip on top of that. However, that gratuity might go in part to the company, so you might give them extra depending on the service. They've got to get out of the car to greet you. They put the bags in the back. It's a nice touch if the guy has a couple of bottles of water and snacks in the car. I had a guy once with a Wet-Nap to wipe your hands and face. Maybe they provide mist, or a phone charger. If I can tell they're going the extra mile, I give them an additional ten or twenty on top of the automatic tip.

- **Airport bag guys.** When I hand my bags to the guys outside the terminal, I give them $10. When I first started out, it was a buck a bag. But now, I just peel a ten off right from the get-go. Even if I have a heavy bag, if I give them ten, they don't charge me the extra hundred because my suitcase is over the limit. The ten-dollar tip saves me ninety.

- **Flight attendants.** I've never tipped a flight attendant. That would be weird.

- **Hotel front guy/valet.** When you arrive at the hotel, you're usually greeted by a doorman or a valet. What I do is give him a ten right out of the car, especially if I'm driving. For ten bucks, he'll park it in the back of the lot. For twenty a day, he'll keep it up top, ready right when you walk out.

- **Bellhops.** Meanwhile, when you pull up, someone is taking your bags out of the car, but he's probably not the guy to bring them to the room. It's confusing. If I don't have a lot of heavy bags and it's just me, I give him a ten. When the bags arrive, if it's a different guy, I give him a ten, too.

- **Housekeeping.** I leave housekeeping $5 per day and $5 per night if they have turndown service. If I don't use a day of service, I leave a $20 because they get paid per room, and if they miss a day because I had the do not disturb sign up, I want to make it up to them.

• **Room service.** An additional tip for room service is bullshit. I don't even like it when they add the tip to the bill. It's presumptuous. If the person is nice and engaged, I might leave a little, but it's not required.

• **The doorman.** If a doorman hails me a cab, he gets $5.

• **Concierge service.** Now, if you call down to the concierge and ask them to bring a toothbrush and toothpaste to your room, the guy who does bring it up to the room gets a five. Could I go downstairs and buy my floss for less than $5? Yes, but if someone does your shopping for you, you've got to tip them.

• **The waiter.** I start at 20 percent, but might go up to 25 or 30 if the service is great. You'd have to shit on the burger for me to give less than 20 percent. If the waiter is a bad server and you don't tip 20 percent, then he or she will say, "See, I knew he wouldn't tip," regardless. I know what they're going through and they deserve the money.

• **The hostess.** To get a table, $100 will guarantee you one no matter where you are in the U.S. If not, get out of there, they suck. The hundge slip has never let me down. If you do it once, you're good for life at some places. I gave $100 at a wine place I go to, and the host will now secure me a table anytime I show up.

If you want to be treated well, give a nice tip. It's not so hard to understand. You don't have to drop twenties left and right, just whatever you can do will be appreciated.

10

COFFEE DATE

I met Chris Mazzilli, co-owner of the Gotham Comedy Club, in 2009 at the Just for Laughs Comedy Festival in Montreal, Canada. At the time, I'd never done his club, I just got introduced to him in the lobby of the Hilton Hotel by a comedian named Steve Byrne. Steve said, "Hey, Chris. This is my friend Sebastian, a really good comedian. He should do your club."

At this point in my career, I had to wonder how the hell everyone else had played New York City but me. How did everyone else know one another? This guy had never heard of me? I felt like I was behind. I wondered why I was always the guy pursuing instead of being chased.

It had been the same when I was trying to meet girls. I always found out too late. I heard the girl I had a crush on in high school also liked me, but I didn't hear this news until I was in college. It was sort of like living in Europe and getting the new movies two years later. Nobody would ever say, "Hey, Sebastian, so-and-so likes you."

My friend in high school Tony Cecala was the exact opposite. We would go out, and women would flock to him like flies on shit. This was only after he turned eighteen. Before then, he was heavy, but he went on a mission to get ripped. He lost forty pounds and changed his name to Anthony. You can't just demand that people call you by your full name all of a sudden because you lose weight. You can't just add the letters back. I'd called him Tony my whole life, and now I had to recalibrate.

So anyway, at a club, he would leave with one girl, plus eight dates lined up for the week. If I was lucky, I would leave with one phone number on a napkin, praying it was real. I had to court the girls, try to charm them with my humor, open their car doors, and prove to them I was a decent guy.

It was always a struggle. Bottom line: No girls or gigs ever fell in my lap. I was never the funny, charismatic guy when meeting girls, never the life of the party. I always wanted to be, but I am just realizing that I have always been reserved and insecure about this. I wanted people to seek me out. I felt like a buffoon if I was trying to sell myself in personal and professional relationships.

But being open went against every ounce of Sicilian blood running through my veins. Sicilians are skeptical and always assume the worst—with good reason. Over centuries, the island was overtaken by the Greeks, the Germans, the Turks, the Normans, the Spanish. The people had to rely on each other for their survival, and they got closed off and distrustful of anyone outside their family (case in point: the Sicilian Corleone family). I know it seems like a contradiction to be a standup comedian who hates to call attention to himself, but that was how I felt. I was like a conch deep in his shell that someone would have to find and pry out.

Over time, I realized that, Sicilian or not, I *had* to put myself out there and be open for the right opportunity to walk in. Or else I'd never get to New York City or move to the next level in my career. Doing standup gave me confidence to be more social, but I had to push it farther, and step into the spotlight.

So back at the Montreal Hilton, Steve fixed me up with Chris. Chris and I talked for a bit, and I guess he got to see my act during the festival. Shortly after that, I got a date at Gotham.

At my first gig there, I just couldn't feel comfortable without supplying a thank-you gift for the staff. I had been there on the other side and I wanted good energy in the room. A little goes a long way with people in the service industry. They work on tips to feel appreciated. Second to a tip is a delicious chocolate cupcake in their mouth. A weekend act comes into town to do a gig, and he leaves behind his reputation with the staff. They will talk about how nice or terrible he was, how much he drank, how he tipped, how friendly he was. This chatter spreads wildly through the saloon doors of the kitchen, to the back hallways of a club, into other clubs and other kitchens, and all the way into the management offices. I knew this, having been on the other side.

So I walked into Gotham with a huge box of Baked by Melissa cupcakes, and I passed them out to everyone who worked there, from the bartenders to the waitstaff to the busboys. I wanted everyone to be happy, and honestly, it was the least I could do.

My mother taught me not to show up at anyone's house empty-handed, and this was just an extension of that. The stakes were high when I arrived at what I consider to be one of the hottest rooms in Manhattan. All the heavyweights performed there, and often showed up unannounced to do a celebrity pop-in, making it a real comedy lover's paradise. On any given night, the audience of 350 might be treated to an impromptu hour with Jerry Seinfeld, Dave Chappelle, Lewis Black, or Chris Rock.

Apparently, the cupcakes worked. I had a great weekend at Gotham, killing it and befriending everyone there. Chris and I became fast friends that weekend, too. He let me know in a very subtle, classy way, that he believed in me and could foresee a big future for me. By the end of the week, he said, "I really like what you do. I'm not trying to poach you at all, but if you're ever unhappy with your current representation, we're here."

It was a refreshing change; someone was noticing and pursuing me. I needed someone who believed in me like this, and for the first time I felt like someone out there was taking notice. I was twelve years into the game. My career was on the upswing, and the next step was to assemble the right team around me. Chris and his brother Steve Mazzilli were part of LEG, a talent management company. They could connect me in the comedy club world and introduce me to people. They also knew the casino business, and would open doors for me to do standup in some big venues.

Back in L.A., I had dinner with the head of LEG, Judi Marmel. While courting me to sign on, she took me to a Hawaiian-themed restaurant across the street from her office. This restaurant was not one you'd consider to be high end, especially given the situation. We still joke about how absent-minded she was to take me there for our first dinner. The restaurant wasn't good, but I knew Judi would be the one to take me to the next level. So, managers, when courting comedians: Don't take them to cheap Hawaiian.

Long story short, I ended up signing on with LEG, working with Chris Mazzilli, his brother Steve, and the L.A. division. I was assigned a day-to-day point person. Most of the junior guys were cape grabbing and in the game for free

Ping-Pong and swag at different events. I demanded that if I were going to stay on with LEG, I wanted to work directly with Judi, the Queen Bee, a woman who would buzz into our meetings and make all the worker bees sit up and try to impress her. I began to call her Buzz Buzz. As I came to learn quickly, she is a tried-and-true ballbuster who has earned a reputation over thirty years of being one of the hardest-working managers in the business. Judi has quarterbacked my career to where it is today. She's orchestrated all the different aspects of it, and is always forward thinking. It's all about momentum, with one thing building up to another. She capitalizes on the moment and turns one good thing into other opportunities. Judi is a no-nonsense woman who really knows the business inside and out. She's exceptional at what she does, and I just want to pay homage to her and say thanks.

I'm a loyal guy, and I like to stay with the people who have worked hard for me all these years, including my team at United Talent Agency. I've been with them for ten years now, and they have given me many opportunities to do movies and TV, as well as touring.

With all these pros in my corner, I got to do more improvs all around the country, as LEG owns the improv chains. LEG also produced my second special, *What's Wrong with People?* which really put me on the map. And none of it would have happened if it weren't for that chance meeting in a hotel lobby in Montreal.

CHRIS AND JERRY Seinfeld have been friends for many years. Chris had mentioned to me on multiple occasions that he knew Jerry would be a huge fan of mine and that it was just a matter of time before he could fix us up.

When I finally did met Jerry, in early 2015, I was head-lining at Gotham. He stopped in to do a set right before I went on. I'd been told he was coming, and I was excited that we were finally going to meet. I introduced myself right before he went on stage. Even though I was so excited to meet him, we are both so anti–small talk, we just said "hi" and "bye" and "maybe I'll see you later." What was I supposed to say? "Hey, man. I am so funny you should watch me and laugh"?

I'd been a Seinfeld fan since I was thirteen, watching Jerry do standup about New York taxi drivers at Dangerfield's (Rodney's comedy club on East 61st Street). I clearly remember seeing him on a Jerry Lewis telethon, doing a bit about taking a shower in somebody else's bathroom and noticing a little hair stuck on a wall: "I don't like showering in other people's showers. There's always a problem with temperature adjustment, and there's always a little hair stuck on the wall. You want to get rid of it, but you don't want to touch it. I don't know how it got up that high in the first place. Maybe it's got a life of its own . . ." (You can hear this dialogue in Jerry's voice easily.)

I'd seen hairs on shower walls, but I never thought of it the way he did. He is a genius at noticing these little absurdities in life, pointing them out, and interpreting them from his own perspective. I respond to that style of observational humor. Jerry and I are on the same wavelength in that way—relatable comedy about familiar, simple things. Plus, his standup is precise and lean. No fat on his jokes. He knows that every word means something in comedy. You're not up there to mumble with nothing phrases and sounds. I hate it when a comedian stalls with "ummm" or "like." I pare down my standup to as few words as possible to get the point across, and I learned that from Jerry.

Like everyone else I knew growing up, I counted the days between episodes of *Seinfeld*. The wackiness, the absurdity, a lot of things going on at once, multiple storylines culminating at the end of a twenty-three-minute sitcom. As a kid, I assumed every person in New York was crazy or hilarious or both—and I totally related it to my own wild, hilarious family. Like Jerry's comedy, mine is based on my life and observations, but it rings true for just about anyone. You don't have to be Italian or from Chicago to get it. I meet fans from all over who tell me, "You're talking about my family," even though, obviously, I'm not. The goal is to transport the audience into your reality regardless of where they come from, to tap into the familiar, the things we all know and feel, and describe it in a funny way.

The audience that night at Gotham had come to see me, but they were also huge Seinfeld fans. The MC announced there was a special guest, and when Jerry walked out, the place went *nuts*, screaming, standing, and cheering. They couldn't believe that Jerry Seinfeld was right there in front of them in this intimate club.

The celebrity pop-in is not unique to Gotham. It's a regular occurrence at the Comedy Store and other popular clubs. Usually, if a big name walks in and wants to do time, he or she goes up right away and the regular lineup gets bumped. It sucked as an up-and-coming comedian, thinking you finally got a prime set time only to get bumped and wind up performing at 2 a.m., after everyone goes home. But that's just the way it works in the comedy world.

As a young comedian, you learn to roll with schedule changes, but an even bigger issue is how you're going to follow a big name with great new material. Anyone would be nervous and ask himself, *How do I segue into my act after the audience is basking in the afterglow of an unexpected encounter with Chris Rock?*

So the whole time Jerry was performing at Gotham, I was backstage thinking, *How do I bridge the gap between his act and mine?* You can't follow up Jerry Seinfeld with, "So where you from? What do you do for a living? I just flew in from Cleveland, and, boy, do I have a crick in my neck."

It was wintertime, and Jerry had a scarf on. It was tied intricately—very stylish, very New York—and he kept it on for the first three minutes of his set. So when I got on stage, I said,

"Give it up for Jerry Seinfeld! You know how confident you got to be to wear a scarf three minutes into your set?" Then I did the physical act of tying the scarf and used the microphone cord as a prop. It just kind of loosened up the crowd, reminded them what my comedy is about, and then, boom, I went into my act.

Usually, after a pop-in, Jerry would leave the club right away, according to Chris. He rarely watched five minutes of anyone. But Jerry stayed for the first forty-five minutes of my set. Lana was there that night and could see him laughing. I was on cloud nine knowing that Jerry had enjoyed my set.

The next night, I was told that Jerry was sending his wife, Jessica, with a group of friends to see me. This made me nervous. It was one thing to perform for Jerry Seinfeld, and another to do it for his wife. I know in my own marriage, if Lana doesn't approve of something, it can send me into a complete spiral. My wife can get into my head like she's the captain of my ship, unconsciously steering my thoughts. If her opinion of something is bad, my thoughts can turn stormy and throw off the whole course of my life without my even knowing it. So I thought that I had to make Jessica Seinfeld laugh to confirm Jerry's opinion of my comedy.

It went well, and I was invited to meet Jessica and her friends after the show. At some point, she put me on the phone with Jerry and we had a nice chat. It occurred to me to ask Jessica for Jerry's number, but I would never do that. It's not my style. I'm the cat; I let people come to me. I let him dictate the connection. The last thing I would ever do is overstep my bounds or make assumptions. From afar, Jerry seemed like the kind of guy who didn't want to get to know anyone and didn't need or want any new friends. (I could relate. It takes a cat to know another cat, and I could see his whiskers from a mile away.) But, as I got to know him, I was surprised at how generous and kind Jerry is. He truly loves what he does, and when he believes in something, he gives his whole heart to it.

The next time I ran into him, it was at Gotham again. I remember talking to him about the business of comedy and keeping the act fresh and how to keep people coming back. He told me the main thing is to do your best material, regardless of whether it's new or old. The job is to make people laugh. (Take note, Dad, and now get off my back about new material!)

As we exited the club, Jerry said, "Hey, do I have your number?"

"No, but here it is. Just don't abuse it," I said.

He then got into his car, which was parked right in front of the club on the street in New York City. This is when it occurred to me that this guy has it all figured out. There had been a street cone holding his spot prior to his arrival. I thought, *Does the club have a cone guy?* How do they determine who is in charge of the cone? Does a panic ensue when Jerry arrives? Is there is a waiter being yelled at: "Drop the buffalo wings! Forget about the pigs in a blanket. *Go get the cone!* He's here!"

This incident alone piqued my interest. It was a small window into Jerry's life. There is an intriguing quality about him. I was not only ecstatic that Jerry Seinfeld and I would possibly be exchanging "Happy Hanukkahs" and "Merry Christmases," but I was also curious about how a man of his stature navigates his way through life.

WHEN YOU'RE A fan of someone who is way up there, and now you have each other's number, it's strange. How do you use it? Jerry's age was somewhere between mine and my father's, so I had no idea how savvy he was with texting.

If I send my father a text, I'm lucky to hear back at all. If I do, it's often indecipherable and sent long after I forgot about the initial text. Here's an example of a recent text exchange between us:

Dad: "1991."

Me: "What is 1991?"

Him: "When I sold Luigi and Salvo." [The salon he owned with his brother.]

Me: "I asked you that two months ago, and I've seen you three times since then, and Mom already answered."

Him: "1991."

Me: "Okay, thx."

With my mom, on the other hand, as soon as I send her a text, a reply bubble appears instantly, as if she were sitting around, waiting on the text. I'm sure she was. If she texts me a question and I don't respond within sixty seconds, I'll get a follow-up message saying, "Hello?" By the time I see the first text, she's sent a string of "hellos" all lined up in unison. If Facebook had need of a news anchor, it could be Rose Anne Maniscalco. She might call me to say, "Did you see the Marinos' kid is having another baby? You know the Marinos."

I would say, "No, Ma, I have no idea who that is."

"Oh, well, anyway their niece Mary got a new car, a Kia, and it looks nice. What do you think of that car?" And then we're talking about the purchasing decisions of some person I don't know or care about. For half an hour.

Mom's Facebook ads are mostly medical equipment and medication because she has looked up so many illnesses while trying to self-diagnose. She goes so deep on Facebook, she has carpal tunnel in her pointer finger solely from pressing the "show more" button.

So I had no idea what to expect about Jerry's phone style. Nowadays, it's a little too aggressive to just pick up the phone and call someone. But since we'd exchanged numbers, I felt like I should just text a short message, like, "Hey, man. So great talking to you. Let's grab a bite next time I'm in New York." And that would be that.

I didn't hear from him for a few months, and then, when

I did, it wasn't direct. His production company contacted my agents with excellent news: Jerry wanted me to appear on *Comedians in Cars Getting Coffee*, his hit web series.

This was huge. It was a Johnny Carson moment to me.

When I was growing up, I would watch Johnny Carson and I always loved it when he invited comics to sit on the couch and talk to him after they finished their sets. It was like being anointed by the king, the ultimate seal of approval with the whole world watching. From that moment on, your life would never be the same. In this day and age, there are so many platforms to be seen on—cable TV, Netflix, YouTube, Instagram, a dozen talk shows. There is no one show that everyone watches like they did with Carson's *Tonight Show*. But, for comedians, there is a show that gives you a sense of validation, an "I've made it" kind of feeling, and that's *Comedians in Cars Getting Coffee*. He only invites comedians he genuinely enjoys talking to—whom he'd want to hang out with in real life. And now it was my turn. I was getting the Carson couch invite—from Seinfeld.

The *Comedians in Cars* concept is like a talk show, except instead of a desk and a couch, the host and the guest are in a car. The ride Jerry chose for our show was an orange 1969 Camaro Z/28, the original Guido muscle car. He said he could see me driving around in it in high school. My real high school car was 1984 Toyota Celica, shit-brown with a brown interior and roll-down windows that doubled as a forearm exerciser.

The only thing that had power in the car was the engine, a robust four-cylinder that went from zero to sixty in two days.

Jerry picked me up at a house in L.A. It wasn't my own house, although I opened the door like I owned the place. It belonged to a friend of the producers. My home in Hollywood was too far from where we were going in Santa Monica. We greeted each other, shook hands, and I realized we were dressed like identical twins in white shirts, navy blazers, and jeans. There were subtle differences: My jeans were skinny and his were sneaker cut; my shirt was a designer tee and his was a button-down. Jerry wore his blue-and-orange Mets Nikes; I wore boots. But standing side by side, it was like we'd called each other to wear matchy-matchy outfits.

Jerry commented on my cologne. He said he didn't wear any. I was taught how to put on cologne by my grandfather. The technique was passed down from generation to generation in the Maniscalco family and it goes as follows: a spritz on each wrist, two in the air, and then a walk through the mist. On the lawn, I showed Jerry how I do it, and he cracked up. I liked how the joke played, and later I included that footage in the video I use before I come out onstage at standup shows. Hey, if you had five seconds of video of yourself making Seinfeld laugh, you'd show it every chance you got, too.

The first five minutes of filming were almost surreal. On the show, it looks like we're just riding around Los Angeles—him driving, me grinning like a chimpanzee in the passenger seat—

with a dash cam and multiple GoPros throughout the car, a guerilla-type production. But in reality, we had a police escort on a motorcycle and a production team in two vans, with three cameramen, a boom guy, and producers riding alongside and behind. Seeing the scope of what it took to make this show floored me.

Jerry's only direction was the same one that I've heard since my earliest days in comedy: "Just be yourself!" He told me to be comfortable and pretend like the eighty-nine people buzzing around us weren't there. I remember him saying it seems a little chaotic in the beginning but I'd get used to it. It took twenty minutes before I felt like I could have a normal conversation. I'm so sensitive to energy, it was hard for me to be natural with all those people hovering. How to ignore the cameras? How can I "be myself" in front of eighty-nine strangers? I can *perform* in front of strangers, but the only time I'm completely myself is with my wife. I'm a different version of myself depending on who I'm with, so I just had to find the one that would shine best in this scenario.

It's common practice for hosts on late-night TV to predetermine what you're going to talk about. The host comes in with a stack of questions and discussion topics that have been worked out ahead of time. A good host makes it seem off the cuff, but it's all arranged so that the comedian can do his or her act within the pretense of a spontaneous conversation. Before

Jerry and I got in the car, he said, "I want to set you up for that joke about taking your shoes off at somebody's house. I'll just weave in a question that leads to that."

He teed me up by talking about how I'm an obsessive groomer, how I like to polish myself up to a brilliant sheen, and we got to talking about slob culture. I ran with it:

> *The airport is a prime example. People put on pajamas to fly. The way I grew up, when you see the world, the world sees you. When did it become appropriate to wear flip-flops to a nice steak dinner? I got to sit there eating a T-bone, looking at some guy's hoof? Put a shoe on!*

That dovetailed perfectly into:

> *We went over for a dinner party last week at some guy's house, and as soon as I walk in, there's like twenty-five pairs of shoes sitting by the doorway. The guy says, "This is a shoe-free environment." So I'm walking around his house with my socks on, meeting people with their socks on. How can you have a conversation with another man, looking at their Gold Toes? I can't do it.*

He said, "Meanwhile, they got a dog dragging his ass around."

I asked about his social life and how his wife has opened him up more. "She has, because she's a normal person," he said. "Just a human being. I have none of that."

I told him, "My wife wants me to smile more. She thinks I have a 'mean resting face.' If I'm not smiling or talking, it looks like I could murder your whole family."

Jerry claimed his wife never saw his true personality. "My real-person personality is nothing but judgment and hostility."

"You can't bring that home."

"No."

"I try to be friendly," I said. "It doesn't work."

"Maybe it's the murderer face."

The entire drive was like that, a volley back and forth of one- or two-liners, light and easy.

I had no idea where we were going until he just pulled into a parking lot of Intelligentsia, an extravagant coffee place where the coffee beans are raised like Kobe beef cows. They go to Guatemala and personally massage each bean for months. It's one of these hipster places where the barista has a handle-bar mustache and all of the customers are on their laptops. If the Wi-Fi went down, the people would flee faster than if the health department condemned it. Modern-day coffeehouses cannot exist without Wi-Fi and vice versa. They have a totally codependent relationship.

We walked in with a production team, three cameras, a boom mic, and a lot of commotion, not to mention a living icon of comedy, a guy who had the most successful show in the history of television—but the customers didn't peel their eyes away from Throwback Thursday posts. I was checking for people's reaction to Jerry, and they didn't care. The president could have skipped in there holding hands with Vladimir Putin, and they would have kept staring at their computer screens. It was eerily quiet, too, like at one of my sets in the early days.

It was not at all what I had expected from being in public with Jerry. No commotion, no nothing. A couple people sneaked peeks, but no one lost their shorts or anything remotely approaching gawkery. In L.A., a celebrity sighting is like seeing a McDonald's on a corner. If it was Cincinnati, they would have had to shut down the streets and bring riot cops. But this was a full-blown production and people literally didn't bat an eye. I was stunned.

Jerry took in this strange environment, too, and said, "The world has turned into the monkey cage. Darting eyes and a little fear." Funny, creepy, and so true.

Only the waiter wasn't too cool for school. He was shy or nervous, rattling the porcelain cups and shaking a bit. Jerry engaged with him to calm him down, asking him what he wanted to do with his life, where he saw himself in twenty years. While they talked, I caught my breath before we picked up the conversation again. We'd gone through all the preplanned stuff, and our talk became more organic: exterminators, growing up

Sicilian, the comedy world. He asked, if I weren't doing comedy, what were my other career options?

I said, "I would be in the hospitality business, although I had a problem with people."

After coffee, we walked around in Venice and popped into a hat store. We spent twenty minutes goofing around, trying on fedoras and cowboy hats (cue the rom-com "shopping montage" soundtrack). For the record, I'm not a hat person. My head is too large. When I wear a hat, it looks like a bottle cap on a watermelon.

I was sure that our day would end there, but Jerry took me to the Tasting Kitchen, an Italian restaurant. It was closed except for us. We sat down, and Jerry looked across the table at me and said, "I've never taken anybody on this show for a glass of wine, but I think it's appropriate. You being Italian, you loving wine, I love wine, let's go get some wine." I played it cool, but now we were speaking my language. It is almost impossible for me to turn down a glass of good wine. Talk about being myself: throw me a glass of Cabernet or Tuscan wine, and there I am, in my element.

Out came the Italian wine, olives, and cheese, and we started talking about our marriages. I told him that Lana is Jewish. I have a joke in my act about the Italian-Jewish connection ("same corporation, different divisions"), and Jerry suggested I call her so he could say hello. I phoned Lana and put her on speaker. By the tone of her voice, I could tell she was surprised and a bit flustered. It goes up a few octaves when she's nervous.

My wife is very supportive of what I do, as well as a huge part of it. The ostensible reason Jerry had suggested the call was "I'm a Jew; she's a Jew. Let's have Jew talk." But I think he knew how much the day meant to me, and that involving my wife would give Lana and me a shared memory, something to savor together later on.

LAST TIME I was in New York, Jerry and I went to dinner at Estiatorio Milos, a Greek restaurant on West 55th Street and one of my favorite places in the city. We were joined by the Mazzilli brothers and George Wallace, a comedian.

If I invite you to dinner, it's a rule for me to pick up the tab. I don't care who the hell you are. I invited Jerry and the whole group to my favorite restaurant, so it was on me.

My dad always carries around a huge knot of bills (pulled from the ceiling), even now when everyone uses cards. He'll say, "What if the credit card doesn't work?" You have to have the amount of cash in your pocket to cover wherever you are going to eat. That was instilled in me from the get-go: always carry cash. And when you have a wad of bills, it's easy to pay for dinner without having a big commotion about it and without having to wait for the check to be brought back and nowadays the need to check your credit card statement to make sure the place didn't rob you or steal your identity.

A lot of people wait until the check is dropped, and then hesitate long enough for someone else to grab it. You have a big song and dance. If you *really* want to pay for a bill, you give the credit card to the guy *before you even sit down* (thank you, Scott Lutgert). Just say, "Make sure that the bill goes on this card." Or you do what I did. After we finished, I got up as if to go to the bathroom and asked the waiter, "Can you bring the bill to me off to the side?"

I went back to the table and said we could go.

Someone asked, "What about the bill?"

"It's taken care of," I said.

Sometimes, like that night, there might be a protest, as in "What are you doing? You don't have to do that."

Oh, but I do. Especially if my companion paid the bill last time. Jerry insisted on picking it up when we had dinner at Mozza in L.A. It was not only my invitation, it was also my turn.

I'm sure he'll get another chance to wrestle me for the bill. It's been three years since I made fun of Jerry's scarf at Gotham, and now I consider him a friend. We've bonded over our two favorite things: food and comedy.

MY BEST FRIENDS aren't part of comedy at all. They're from the old days, high school and college. They're working-class guys, real estate agents, housepainters, and money managers. They've been with me this whole time. When they used to come to my shows out of town, we were all so broke, we'd share one hotel room. So now, I get comped enough rooms at a casino for all of them to have their own, plus a steak dinner, too. I love to share what I'm doing with my family and old friends. That's where I get my enjoyment. No matter what, I can count on these guys to keep me grounded and rip me to shreds. These days, we're in better hotel rooms, but the relationships haven't changed.

People can get a big head in this business. Yes, I have an actual big head physically, but I'm so turned off by big egos. There are no guarantees in comedy, and I've noticed that the bigger people's heads, the more they lose sight of the reason they're here in the first place. I love what I do; that's what's important to me. I keep my head down and just do what I've been doing for nineteen years: booking gigs, traveling, working on my material. I've picked up some momentum, but it's happened over a long time. It's not like I was doing bowling alleys yesterday, and today it's Caesar's Palace. Every year, my road has gotten smoother. More people come out to see me. More opportunities are cropping up. The progress has been so gradual that when I glance at the speedometer, I'm shocked to see that I'm doing 110.

It's my tendency to be observant, but not necessarily introspective. When I take time to slow down and reflect, like looking in the rearview mirror of life—or writing a book about the road I've traveled—it only makes me want to turn back around, face forward, and go faster. I have a deep-seated fear of resting in one place. No amount of validation, even from Jerry Seinfeld, is going to make me feel complacent, slow down, or stop.

My wife says that I'm superstitious about it. If I were to say to myself, "Wow, you're doing great," it'd be a jinx. She's right. I do believe that if I relished my success at all, even for a minute, I'd hit a wall and it would be over. I'll probably never relax about where I am or where I'm headed.

In the long run, which, hopefully, we're all on, I don't want to be built for comfort, like a Cadillac. I don't care about being built for speed, like a Camaro.

I want to be built *to last*, like a Camry.

11

CHIP

Lana and I started trying to have a baby right after a vacation in Greece and Turkey. We felt we needed to get some travel under our belts before jumping into parenthood. Lana got pregnant immediately—we couldn't believe it, we'd just begun trying—and we were over the moon.

We wanted to tell everybody, but we knew about the rule that you should wait twelve weeks before you share the news because of the possibility of a miscarriage. We were too excited, though; we couldn't hold off. We arrived in Naples for Christmas at her parents' house. Her whole family was there, and it seemed a shame to wait another month and a half to tell them over the phone when we could make the big announcement in person. The only issue was that she was so early on, and the doctor was a little hesitant about whether it was going to be a viable pregnancy. But we said, "Screw that," and felt optimistic.

The idea was to tell our families by catching them off guard with some kind of clever Photoshopped meme. I could have re-cycled that mailing I sent to agents and directors when I arrived in L.A., something like, "Coming soon! Baby Maniscalco!" But I'd come a long way since then, and now I had better ideas and just the guy to pull it off.

Steve Mitrano makes memes for my social media ac-counts, to publicize gigs and podcasts by transposing my head into recognizable settings and in strange situations. I didn't find Steve; he found me. He would share his memes of me on social media, and they caught my eye. They were so well done, spot-on—and funny. When I started noticing and loving his work, I thought Steve was just a fan with phenomenal talent. In fact, he's an Emmy-winning graphic artist in the news field. He was just doing memes of me for fun. I was really impressed that he could combine his talent with my comedy to make these incredible images, and I had to make him part of my team.

Lana said, "Hey, Mom, look at this new thing Sebastian is doing." We often shared all sorts of career stuff with Lana's family, so it didn't seem unusual for me to pull up an image on the computer to show them. They looked at the meme of Lana painting a picture of a baby whose face was a combination of our features. I was expecting cheers, tears, an emotional explosion. My wife's family was definitely excited, but their reaction was subdued, like, "Congrats! Great news!"

Over the next week, Lana had some signs that the pregnancy might not be a go. I'll spare you the details, but since we had shared the news with her family, and we wanted to remain optimistic, we decided to tell my family, too. Everyone was going to be together in L.A. for New Year's, so we would do it then.

We pulled the same trick on my family with the meme. Their reaction was just a little different from Lana's family.

My father did his signature laugh-yell that comes out in every emotional scenario, because he doesn't know how to respond. It's just a lot of teeth.

My mom screamed, rattling the windows with the volume.

Jessica yelled (like mother, like daughter), right before she started crying, which set off Talia, my five-year-old niece. She was so startled at the intense volume in my sister's voice, she threw herself on the couch crying. Then I started crying, too, because it's how I do. Everyone in the house was hugging, weeping, jumping up and down, clapping like they had just won an all-expenses-paid trip to Jamaica on *Family Feud*. A lot of shit went down in the living room. Lana was a bit quiet, because at this point, she was feeling pretty hesitant that everything was okay.

She was right. A week later, Lana wasn't feeling well. We Googled her symptoms and it was okay, unless it got worse.

Over the course of the day, however, we couldn't write off what was happening to her as "normal." We'd moved into "call your doctor immediately" territory.

Losing that pregnancy was hard, and we grieved. But we both took comfort in the idea that this particular one, for whatever reason, was not meant to be. As far as miscarriages go, it was the best of all possible situations. It happened very early in the pregnancy and resolved on its own. Lana didn't suffer physical pain. And she was only thirty-two. We had plenty of time to try again. The hardest part was calling our families with the bad news only a week after we'd delivered the good news. Our families reacted the same way, nothing but positivity, love, support, and encouragement.

I'm not even sure the second miscarriage counts. We are the type of couple that can't wait for anything. If I get Lana a Christmas gift in November, I have to run home and give it to her within two hours. If I have a surprise for her, I cannot hold it in, and vice versa. I think Lana was doing a pregnancy test just about every hour. Every CVS and Rite Aid within a five-mile radius was cleared out of e.p.ts and First Response tests because of us. One day, the sticks had a faint double line in the window. The next day, the line was gone. If we hadn't been testing obsessively, we might never have known or even gotten our hopes up.

So now we were oh for two, but contrary to my usual default setting, I wasn't worried. I headed off any anxiety by trying to figure out how to make a miscarriage story funny. I don't touch a lot of social issues or politics in my standup, leaving those topics to people who are better informed than me. But in my act I am drawn to dealing with awkward and awful situations in one's personal life, and the puzzle of how to turn tragedy into comedy. What would be the angle? How could I tell a joke about illness, death, or divorce? What observations could I make about miscarriage that other people would relate to and laugh at? It's not like Lana and I were the only people dealing with it. Serial miscarriage is devastating and frustrating, and when it's happening to you, it is all you can think about. But people don't talk about it. First, you keep the pregnancy a secret for twelve weeks. If you don't get that far, you have a second secret on top of the first. Since a miscarriage is sad and upsetting—and rolled up with self-blame and feelings of inadequacy—you swallow the bad feelings instead of airing them out.

Sometimes, it's better to leave bad experiences untouched. Let it alone. But for me, as a comedian, my mind automatically goes there. How could I turn a sadness like that into something funny in any way, shape, or form? I'd be airing it out for my own sake, but also for anyone who'd been there, too. I haven't worked our miscarriages into my act yet. I may never. But it's worth thinking about.

After the second false alarm, Lana's ob-gyn told us to wait before we tried again. She said that Lana's body needed to recover and reset itself to be ready for a new pregnancy.

"How long do we have to wait?" asked Lana.

The doctor said, "Until after you have a normal cycle, which could possibly be a few months or more."

It seemed like a long wait. Too long. Another doctor told Lana it was fine to go ahead and try. We didn't *intend* to go against her ob-gyn's orders, but we figured you can plan on it all day long, but if and when the timing is right, it will happen.

Literally three weeks after the doctor told us not to try, Lana said at breakfast that morning, "I think I'm pregnant."

Immediately, I drove to the nearest pharmacy and filled up a basket with dozens of pregnancy tests. I had to get the digital one, the one that says "pregnant," instead of the ones with the lines. These are not clear enough for me. In a world of emojis, I think they need to come out with the iPreg, an app where you urinate on the camera lens, and if you're pregnant, a digital infant will dance across the screen. Drugstore tests are too subtle and need an update!

Lana basically spent the morning on the toilet, drinking water and peeing on every stick in the bag. Parallel lines, plus sign, they all said the same thing: *definitely* pregnant.

We were thrilled, but based on prior experiences, we didn't let our hopes get too high. We wanted to be excited, but we knew the harsh truth about what could happen. I wouldn't say we were pessimistic, more like cautiously optimistic. We lived for three whole months in that limbo between allowing yourself to be happy and keeping your emotions in check. We told no one close to us. The only people besides the doctor who knew were the nail lady at Pampered Hands (Lana had to make sure she didn't use any harmful products), her Pilates teacher (no harmful exercises), and the guy at the juice shop (no harmful ingredients). We got the official go-ahead at eleven weeks, along with the gender, a girl! Lana intended to wait three days until she saw her mother in person, but who were we kidding? We FaceTimed her mom immediately and then shared the news with the rest of our family and friends.

Our next big project was in development. We were having a baby!

IF ONE PERSON in a relationship goes on a diet, it'll never work. It has to be both of you.

Once, I told Lana I wanted to do a juice cleanse, and she said, "But I don't want to." I wasn't asking *her* to do it, but by her logic, if I did a weeklong juice cleanse, we wouldn't be able to go out to restaurants. We wouldn't cook together, which we love to do, or have wine at night. Forget dinner dates with friends, or sitting around the kitchen table with coffee. I wouldn't have the energy to take long walks or go for a run with her. By doing a cleanse, I'd be depriving her and us of the things we enjoy doing together.

By the same token, if one person is eating no-holds-barred, including stuff she'd typically avoided like ice cream and doughnuts, then the other person has to eat it all, too. I made the decision early on in the pregnancy that I'd partake. So if Lana said to me, "I'm going to order some ice cream to be delivered. You want?" The answer was "Yes!"

Ordering ice cream at night became a pattern during the pregnancy. If a wife is going to have a bowl of it in bed at 9 p.m., then, as a good husband, you better be right there next to her. Pregnancy gave me the excuse to feel liberated to eat whatever I wanted without guilt. There were no juice cleanses during this time to say the least. We basically did a world tour of cuisines from the comfort of our home, thanks to Postmates, a delivery service where you can get any meal from any restaurant brought to your door.

Lana's only food restriction was no raw fish or rare meat. So when she got the craving for sushi, we'd order from Nobu, and she'd have rolls of cooked fish like eel and shrimp. She often craved steak, so I had recently learned how to cook it properly. I used to just throw a steak on the grill, and it always came out uneven. The outside would burn, and the inside was raw. I researched online the perfect method for getting a nicely seared, evenly cooked medium rare steak by doing it slow at a low temperature to allow the meat to retain the juices. My recipe:

Step one: Preheat the oven to 275 degrees.
Step two: Season the steak with salt and pepper.

Step three: Put it in an oven-safe pan and roast for
forty-five minutes.

Step four: Take it out and let it rest for fifteen minutes.

Step five: Sear the meat on a dry, hot cast iron pan—no
oil, no butter—for two minutes on each side.

Always juicy and delicious. Try it!

Our favorite nighttime snack is popcorn. My wife makes
an unbelievable batch in the Whirley Pop (a pot with a churner
inside for perfect popping). She puts a little vegetable oil in the
pot, heats it up, and then pours in Boulder Popcorn's Cambria's
Cream small kernels, and starts whirling. When it's done, it
goes in a bowl, lightly salted. During the pregnancy, we were
knocking down bowls of it every night.

I know some expectant fathers complain behind their
wives' backs about how much they're packing away. I was *glad*
Lana was indulging! I figured, if she was eating, the baby was
eating, too. And so was I! The results were all too predictable:
When Serafina was born in April 2016, I was the heaviest
I'd ever been, at 208 pounds. I gained 23 pounds during the
nine months of Lana's pregnancy, which was nearly the same
amount she gained. (I'm down to 198. Only 13 pounds to go.
Ideally, I'll lose it before Lana gets pregnant again, before I go
right back up.)

Our pregnancy was all about staying home and eating,

watching ourselves get bigger, and charting the baby's growth. I went to every doctor's visit and saw each sonogram. I would make commentary videos to send around. I was fascinated by the heartbeat and the changes on the monitor from visit to visit. Lana subscribed to a pregnancy website that described the baby's size in utero week to week. "At eight weeks, the baby is the size of a clove of garlic." "At twelve weeks, the baby is the size of a lime." "At sixteen weeks, the baby is the size of an avocado." Why was I suddenly craving guacamole?

TOWARD THE MIDDLE of the pregnancy, we hired a doula. A doula, in case you didn't know, is a woman who talks you through the pregnancy and childbirth, explains things, answers questions, and gives you emotional support.

I asked my wife, "Is the doula a nurse?"

"No," she said.

"Is she a doctor?"

"No."

"Is she a trained expert?"

"She's had a few kids of her own."

"And how much does this cost?"

"I'm not sure. But it's priceless!"

What? I knew better than to argue with a pregnant woman, so I just casually asked if we really needed a doula, and Lana insisted that yes, we did. My wife's family does a lot of things that are unfamiliar to me. They've got staff. They hire a gardener, a housekeeper, and, apparently, a doula. Goes without saying that when I was born, the doula was my mom.

So this woman shows up at the house with yoga balls and diagrams of the female reproductive system. The icing on the cake was the stuffed animal placenta. She showed us different techniques to help with the birthing process and gave us an overview of how the delivery might go down. Lana and I acted like thirteen-year-olds in sex ed. We literally were dying laughing the entire time.

The doula was around thirty-eight and was very soothing, a real earth mother type. Lana intended to try to give birth without drugs, so the doula taught her techniques to lessen the pain of childbirth, and she had Lana do exercises on the yoga ball. She'd sit on it and spread her legs, to take pressure off the hips, and roll around on it. For weeks, the doula came over and taught Lana a bunch of techniques. Would any of them work? We'd have to wait until she went into labor to find out. I sat there watching all of this, thinking it was a scam. When my mom gave birth to me—I was ten and a half pounds—she had no drugs, no doula, and barely a husband.

Lana's due date was May 1, but on April 24, a week early, the doctor said she was concerned about Lana's fluid levels. If they got too high, the baby could be in danger. She suggested inducing labor, and Lana was all for it at that point. My wife was ready for the baby to come out and didn't need to wait one more week for labor to start naturally. So before it even started, the "no drugs" labor was getting a medical intervention.

We didn't go over that decision with the doula. There was nothing to discuss. If the baby was at risk at all, the all-natural plan got thrown out the window. We arrived at Cedars Sinai Hospital at 12:40 p.m., Lana was treated with Cervidil to get the process started, along with a Foley balloon in her cervix to open it up. I realized that all the discussion and planning about how the birth was going to go was really just something to do to prepare mentally. When it came down to the pure physical labor, none of that mattered, or even came into play.

Lana started having bad contractions right away after she was induced, but she wanted to hold out as long as she could without an epidural. After an hour, she said, "This is ridiculous. I need something."

"The yoga ball?" I asked.

"Fuck the yoga ball," she said. "I need the epidural!"

My wife is extremely strong and tough. She can run for five miles straight uphill, and she never mentions anything about pain. So for her to say she needed relief told me that she was in agony. I knew the contractions were killing her, and all I could do was stand there and watch it happen. I wanted to help, but how? Every father must feel as frustrated and powerless as I did in that room. I couldn't wait for the anesthesiologist to show up with the needle. When he finally arrived, I was almost as relieved as Lana.

I'd heard that the epidural needle was six inches long. It had to penetrate her skin and muscle and go between vertebrae. Medicine was injected into the spinal cord, and any pain she felt below the waist would be gone.

My mother didn't have an epidural. Maybe they gave her a leather strap to bite down on, I don't know. In those days, fathers weren't in the delivery room either. Matter of fact, I think my father was at the salon in the middle of a perm. I wasn't going anywhere, but that didn't mean I wanted to watch the needle go into Lana. They put a sheet up to keep the area sterile, and I stayed on the other side of it. I guess I could have been the dork who says, "I'm curious how it all works. Can I watch the procedure?" *No way.* If I'd have seen the procedure, I might have passed out, and then there would have been two patients in the room.

Lana's relief was immediate. The pain wasn't completely gone, she said, but it was a lot better. She got a "walking epidural," so she could get out of the bed and move if she needed to go to the bathroom. I was so relieved that my wife was comfortable, I could finally relax.

Believe it or not, after the epidural, we actually slept for a few hours, Lana in the bed and me on the couch in the hospital room. I remember my mother-in-law shaking me awake to tell me that things were progressing fast, and that it was almost time.

Based on what I'd seen in movies and on TV, I'd thought

the room was going to be packed like a sold-out show, with ten or twelve people in there, nurses running around, orderlies, candy stripers. But it was nothing like that. There was just the doctor, two nurses, Lana, me, and my mother-in-law, Simone. Lana started to push, and in my head, I was thinking, *Where is everyone? Who's working the monitor? Who's going to dab Lana's brow with a cold compress?*

By now, the contractions were coming every two minutes. Lana would say, "I feel one coming," and the graph on the screen would confirm that she was accurate.

"Push!" the doctor said. "Push like you're taking a poop!"

So she'd push and do the breathing, and when the contraction subsided, she'd catch her breath and we would hang out and talk about things like the stock market or if we needed a few more throw pillows on the couch. Then *push push push push*, and I asked, "What are you in the mood for for dinner? I'm sort of in the mood for tacos. Or ramen."

Lana said, "As long as it's not hospital food! *Okay, here comes another.*"

Then *push push push push*, and relax. "Hey, baby," I asked, "did you talk to the gardener about our agave plant?"

"Yeah, we need to change the sprinkler settings," she said. "It's getting too much water."

"Okay, great, honey. I'll get right on that."

"*Oh, I think I feel another one . . .*" Push push push push . . .

Like that. Shockingly casual.

I also thought, based on movies, that two pushes would do it and the baby would just shoot out. Not true. After ten cycles of pushing, I stopped counting. I thought there'd be chaos and people shouting out hospital code and monitor readings. It was actually extremely quiet in there.

I remember I was holding my wife's foot and the nurse was holding the other one. During one contraction in the beginning, I was looking up at Lana's face and she said, "You can't look at me while I'm doing this." She made Simone and me look out the window, because she said it's too awkward for us to see her shit face.

So I kept on holding her foot, and when she had a contraction, I'd look out the window. Then, she'd say, "Okay, done," the contraction passed, and I could look at her again. I kept this up, gazing out the window like a fool and then back at her, for an hour and a half. I remember seeing the Hollywood sign out the window and thinking, *Wow, I came out here eighteen years ago with nothing, wanting to give the comedy business a try. Never did I imagine I would be looking at that sign and holding my wife's swollen ankles while my daughter's head was halfway out of her vagina.*

When the baby crowned, I wasn't sure I wanted to watch. But I looked anyway, and saw Serafina's head emerge. It was just the top at first, and then the whole cranium popped out. The doula had warned us that the baby's soft skull sort of collapsed to fit through the birth canal. Serafina was a Conehead.

I thought, *Holy shit, that is a huge head!* Was it going to stay that way? Lana needed to plan some hairstyles that would flatter a pointy head.

A couple pushes later, the body came out. *That's my daughter*, I thought, and started bawling. *Bawling*. At moments like that, I can't control my feelings—and why would I want to? Seeing my daughter's birth was beautiful, unforgettable. I can only describe it as uncontrollable joy.

The nurses and doctor start wiping her down, getting the mucus out of her nose and mouth, cleaning off her little body. It happened really fast. Then the doctor put a pair of scissors in my hand and told me to cut the umbilical cord. I was nervous to do it, thinking it might hurt Lana or Serafina, but I did it anyway, while still ugly crying with my mouth open. When I realized what the texture was like, I thought, *I got this.* The texture felt just like a piece of calamari.

Then the baby was on Lana's chest, and I circled them both with my arms. Our relatives knew the gender, but we hadn't told anyone the name: Serafina Simone. Lana had designed a little embroidered patch that was sewn onto a little cotton hat. Oh, that's right, the embroidery guy also knew the name, and Lana made him swear to secrecy. I had the hat in my pocket and put it on the baby's head. At that moment, my mother-in-law found out we'd named our daughter after her. Needless to say, she started bawling, too.

WE HIRED KARRIE, a night nurse, to educate us on what to expect—sleep training, bottles, bathing, everything. She was basically our baby therapist. She and Lana would talk for hours every night about all things infant.

To be honest with you, at first I was uncomfortable with Karrie being there. A stranger sleeping on the couch in my newborn baby's room? Shouldn't we be going through the trials and tribulations of raising the baby by ourselves? That was how my parents did it. But then again, unlike Mom and Dad, Lana and I didn't have a lot of family around to help us. My mother had moved to Los Angeles by then, but she lived forty-five minutes away, not "Mom, I need you *now!*" distance. And regardless, my mom is "fun grandma." She comes to play, not to implement schedules. When you don't have immediate assistance, you hire people. Despite my initial hesitation, I quickly came to see Karrie as a blessing. She taught us what we needed to know and did whatever she could to help us get a decent night's sleep.

Being a father played into all of my anxieties. As a new parent, you're always concerned. *Should we swaddle the baby? Should the baby be doing that? Is that a rash? What's that mark on her cheek? What does all that* mean? Having a pro right there in our house to bounce stuff off eased our way into parenthood. Any questions my wife had during the day about breast-feeding, napping, and you name it, were bounced off Karrie via text or phone call or when she came in. She obviously knew what she was doing. Karrie had Serafina sleeping through the night at six weeks old.

During our non-sleeping hours, we didn't leave the baby's side. Lana was breast-feeding, so she was literally attached to Serafina every two hours. My father had been old school, leaving the grosser parts of parenthood—diaper changing, cleaning spit up—to my mom. I was not going to emulate my father in that way. I did it all. One morning, I was bringing Serafina to Lana for her morning feed. I had no shirt on and Serafina latched onto my nipple. I didn't know how to take this, but I laughed it off and did extra bench presses for the next two weeks.

As a father you have to find your role. My role became the butler to my wife. Lana would sit down to breast-feed and I would get her all of the things she needed one by one. She would say, "Babe, can you please bring me my phone and a water?"

"Right away, ma'am," I'd say.

As soon as I would sit down, she would throw me another "Hey, baby."

"Yes, honey?"

"Can you please grab the frozen grapes?"

"Right away, my love."

I didn't dare say no, because she had literally grown this magical little human in her belly and was giving Serafina all of the nutrients she needed to keep growing. I really came to appreciate and understand the role of a mother, and being her butler was the least I could do.

If Lana and I went into a different room when Serafina was napping, we watched her on our phones via the live streaming app that connected to the Nest camera by her crib. Whenever I was out of the house for any reason, I found myself checking the baby camera app constantly. It was addicting. At any time I could look at my daughter and see that she was safe.

Serafina was ten days old when we decided to go have our first dinner out. I knew plenty of people who, after they became parents, never carved out time for themselves. We once met this couple for dinner and they said, "This is the first time we've been out since the baby was born a year and a half ago."

I said, "You couldn't get a babysitter?"

My buddy said, "Babysitters are expensive."

I almost said, "You think babysitters are expensive, how about marriage counselors?"

We'd stayed in a lot more than usual during the pregnancy, and now I wanted to go out. It's important to get a little break. Our lives were centered around the baby, but if we didn't get a few hours to detach once in a while, we were going to go nuts. I said to Lana, "Why not go out to eat instead of sitting here, watching the baby sleep? We have the help."

So Lana, my mother, and I went to Il Piccolino for dinner. It was only a five-minute drive from our house. As soon as we sat down, Lana opened the app and checked the baby. In the grainy black-and-white picture, it looked like a blanket was covering the baby's face.

We called Karrie, but she didn't answer. *Where the fuck is she? Sleeping? Does Karrie have a blanket over her head, too?* I was boiling, but trying not to stress Lana out too much. We even did the walkie-talkie through the Nest cam, but we were getting no response. We told each other, "I'm sure it's fine," and tried to go on with our dinner, but Lana was crawling out of her skin.

She said, "What do we do?" We tried calling and texting a few more times to no avail. There was no way we could continue our dinner assuming everything was okay.

I told Lana, "Go home and check on the baby. We'll stay here."

About ten minutes later, my mother and I watched on my phone as Lana walked into the baby's room and checked the crib. She texted, "All good. It was just the angle of the camera that made it look as if the blanket was over her face." When Lana got back to the restaurant, she told us that Karrie had turned off her ringer to let the baby sleep. We all decided from then on that the ringer was on when we were out.

My mother said, "When you were a baby, you didn't have a camera in your room."

No kidding, Ma. Just ask our neighbors from back in the day.

MY PARENTS HAD no idea what was going on in my room after they tucked me in. One time when I was around ten, I sleepwalked out the screen door, hopped a short fence, and ran through dewy grass in my Pittsburgh Steelers pajamas. I think I was dreaming about being Franco Harris running down the field, but I was running down Shag Bark Lane to my next-door neighbors Bonnie and Frank's house. My parents had no idea that I was even gone.

Bonnie was forty years old at the time. I knocked on her door and she answered in her negligee. Theirs was the house in the neighborhood that nobody ever saw the inside of. Maybe it was the mystery that lured me there in my sleep. So she invited me in. I do remember getting a glimpse into their entryway, and seeing two metal armored knights standing there like something out of medieval times. As I progressed through the house, it looked like a mix of King Arthur and *Scarface*, lots of black and red with dim lighting. She took me into her bedroom with a gold rotary phone and gold silk sheets on the bed. It looked like the movie producer's bedroom in *The Godfather*. The only thing that was missing was a horse's head.

My father is the type of sleeper where he didn't budge until his internal alarm clock woke him up for work. My parents were sound asleep, comfortable. They had a waterbed. It had a mirrored canopy. I think my dad got a deal on it from a porno set clearance sale.

When you're a kid, you just think the mirrored bed is sort

of cool. To this day, I've never had a conversation with my parents about this. How do you even bring that up over breakfast? "Hey, Mom. Do you like the mirrored bed because . . . er, nevermind. Um, can you pass the biscuits?"

So how this went down was Bonnie called my house and said to my mom, "Do you know your son is in my bedroom right now?"

Needless to say, my parents were clueless that Bonnie and I were hanging out in our PJs in her bedroom next door.

Mom said, "What do you mean? Nobody in the Arlington Heights vicinity has ever made it past your welcome mat! I've been dying to see the inside of your house for fifteen years! How did Sebastian get an invite?"

"Rose, he didn't," said Bonnie. "He sleepwalked over here. Can you come get him, please?"

"Only if you show me your front room!"

That will not happen with Serafina, because we will get an alert if she so much as twitches. Obviously, human babies have survived until adulthood without cameras in their faces 24/7. But the technology exists now, so we were going to use it. I knew it was intrusive, and might cause more anxiety than it quelled, but I liked being able to look at my baby to see what she was doing when I was away from home. And that was how we were going to raise her.

I realized that dinners out from now on were going to be with phones on the table and camera apps open. Our lives were completely changed. We'd been to this restaurant millions of times, not a care in the world. Before, we'd have pasta and a glass of wine and talk to each other. Now, as soon as we sat down, we were glued to the app, trying to see breathing movements. Before, we'd linger between courses. Now Lana raced home to check the baby.

Sometimes, as a new parent, you need to be crazy. You need to check in. You assume nothing. Your baby is your heart existing outside your body. This is a whole new level of responsibility I'd never had before, and it hit me full force. It took me forty-three years to get here, but I was ready for this.

WHEN SERAFINA SMILES, she looks like Lana. When she's annoyed with people, she looks like me. When I'm there, Lana and I wake the baby up together. As soon as she sees us, she starts smiling and kicking her feet and flailing her arms in cheer. I jump out of bed to see that. In my previous life, I would never get out of bed so early for anything. But the promise of seeing Serafina focus in and freak out in happiness is the best alarm clock in the world. Even if she's hungry or has gas and starts crying, it's exciting to see this tiny person expressing herself with such gusto.

Making people laugh has long been my connection to humanity. If I can make you smile or crack up, we are bonded, at least for the moment. I feel the energy pass between us. When

I play a large venue like Mohegan Sun, I feel that energy times ten thousand.

Well, making Serafina laugh is like ten thousand Mohegan Suns. It's the greatest joy of my life. She smiles at me, and I'm done. I travel all of the time for work, and it has become painful to leave home. I was in New York recently to scope out some locations for my next special, and every second I wasn't in a meeting, I played a video Lana sent me of Serafina in the little activity chair we call her desk, laughing. I put it on a loop and lost an hour before I realized what had happened. Since I had a baby, it's been hard to get anything done.

My friends with older kids tell me to enjoy every moment. I already have a sense that it's going by too fast. One day, she lifts her head. The next, she rolls over. The next, she's off to college. Right now, she might be grabbing my shirt and spitting up on my shoulder, but in a blink, she will be asking me, "Dad, aren't you embarrassed?" I can't wait to get to know this tiny person who already can make me melt with the way she bats her eyes.

And now I'm welling up again.

I'm new at this, but I have figured out a few things about fatherhood: It has doubled my joy—and anxiety. It's put a permanent lump in my throat. And it involves a lot of crying—by me.

12

ACTING CHOPS

In the last few years, I've noticed that I'm getting a lot of calls about acting. Ironically, when I first started out as a performer, acting was what convinced me to go west to L.A. I wanted to do standup, but all of my experience was in theater.

After graduating college, I was in a very different boat than my friends. They'd lined up jobs in the fields they majored in. Basically, nothing in my life had been planned besides the dream of being a comedian. I majored in corporate organizational communications. The reason I majored in this was because it was the only major that didn't require a test to get in.

Out of college, I had been working as a temp at the United Airlines Employees Credit Union. My job was to enter codes for preordered specialty meals into the system. There is nothing more boring than entering in the code for an airline meal ordered by a stranger in 32B. If you flew on United Airlines in the early '90s and received Salisbury steak instead of the vegetarian meal you requested, it was because I was working the graveyard shift and did not give a shit. The last thing I was concerned about was who was pissed off about the meal mix-up on the way to Dulles International.

During this job hell, I saw an ad in a local paper looking for actors to appear in an interactive dinner theater production in Chicago. I had never done anything like that before, but sometimes, when you don't know what to expect, you're better off.

It was for a show called *Joey and Mary's Irish Italian Comedy Wedding*, like *Tony and Tina's Wedding*, but with an Irish twist. I auditioned for the part of the best man, Gino Cappellini. I went into the audition and knocked it out of the park just being me. I had no fear or expectations. I just did it because I thought it would be fun, and they gave me the part in the room. I took my place in a cast of real theater actors who were in the Steppenwolf Theatre Company, a prestigious notch on any actor's belt. While these people were studying acting meticulously, I was pretending to care about my corporate organizational communications degree, which must have indirectly given me *some* acting chops.

I had no formal acting training at all, but what I did have was the bluster of youth and positive prior experience being on stage in front of a large group of people and making them laugh. Back in college, there was this bodybuilding contest called Greek Physique. All the fraternities and sororities would do a skit and then one representative from each house would come out and pose. I wasn't the bodybuilder for my frat, but I did write the skit and MC the event, and I killed it. I figured *Joey and Mary's Wedding* would be an extension of that.

I was still living at my parents' house in the burbs, so I had to drive to the city for daily rehearsals. The director's plan was to do shows at different banquet halls around the Chicago area. We'd go into a catering hall in, say, Addison, Illinois, turn the space into a wedding set—tables, a DJ, a cake, flowers—and put on the show.

If you haven't experienced interactive dinner theater, you really need to do it once. The concept is that you are attending a real wedding reception as a guest, and you sit at an assigned seat at a table with other people, some of whom are actors. The more you get into it and play along, the more fun you'll have.

There was a loose script, but pretty much it was up to each actor to get the people involved in the drama. I would jump right in at my table with typical wedding icebreakers, like "Which side are you on? I haven't seen you in the family, so you must be with the bride." Or I'd say to a woman, "I saw you looking at me but I got a girlfriend, so back off." You had to be willing to play with me for the joke to work, but a lot of people wouldn't say anything. They'd get embarrassed and I—excuse me, *Gino Cappellini*—would have to monopolize the conversation.

There's a hilarious episode of *Curb Your Enthusiasm* when Larry David went to an interactive show like this, and he knew one of the actors. He kept trying to get the guy to break character. When they were in the bathroom together, Larry said, "So, John, how you been?"

The guy said, "Who's John?" Larry wouldn't let it go, and chaos ensued.

When my family came to the show, it was a real challenge for me to stay in character. I'd see my mom was on the dance floor and I'd have to say, "Hey, how you doing? I'm Gino Cappellini." She'd crack up, and I'd say, "What's so funny? I got something in my teeth?" In the middle of the evening, the Irish brother of the groom and I broke out into a dance number, and we always brought down the house. We did twelve Saturday night shows in a row. Gino had a girlfriend named Jodie, played by an actress I got to be friends with, and we'd go out with the rest of the cast after a show to party at somebody's house, at a bar, or what have you.

I had a ball doing the show. It was an unforgettable summer for a twenty-two-year-old kid. But, as far as acting goes, I wouldn't say that I learned a lot. Maybe I picked up more than I would have in doing improv, but not much. There was no dialogue to memorize. My costume was a tux. All I had to do was eat and talk (and dance), skills that were already in my wheelhouse. It got my feet wet in dealing with an ensemble of actors and actresses, and I outshined a lot of them. I consistently made people laugh. I thought, *I can perform. I can make people happy.* The whole experience spurred me to pursue performing for real. I'd been thinking about moving to Los Angeles for months, but I hadn't been able to pull the trigger. Getting the Gino role and doing it well gave me the confidence to say, "I might have something here. I think performing could be a career."

It's not like I was landing any other jobs at the time. The writing was on the wall early that I was not cut out for a cubicle. I thought it was because I wasn't a "good fit" at the Chicago Convention Hall Career Day. In hindsight, I think what turned off potential employers was my metallic silver double-breasted three-piece suit with a red handkerchief and matching red tie from Taylor Street, while everyone else was in a navy business suit and getting hired left and right. I looked like John Travolta from *Saturday Night Fever* going out on Career Day. I had no guidance. Nobody put me in check. My father thought I looked sharp and my mother thought I would get a career as a model.

After landing nothing at Career Day, I began thumbing through the newspapers, and the ads for musical theater kept glaring at me. I just felt bad for my parents, because their friends and neighbors got to brag about the cush jobs their kids were landing. Mine would have to act as if they were proud that I was making less than minimum wage at a part-time gig, after they'd gone through two years of what they called "mall withdrawal" to save up to put me through college. Most parents had an education fund for their children so that when the time came, it was ready to roll. Mine began saving three weeks before orientation.

The best part about my family is that there is a lot of love, no pressure, and we go with the flow. My parents were supportive of my *Joey and Mary* gig, and, in all honesty, I *was* the star of the show. This didn't make me think, *Next stop, Scorsese!* But the summer as Gino did give me a boost and motivate me to go west. It only made sense. I booked it right off the bat and then kept up with serious, veteran actors.

Speaking of the professionals in the cast, I saw the guy who played Joey in New York about three years ago at Eataly, an Italian food marketplace, where he was selling coffee beans. Twenty years ago, we had the same dream and were on the same path together. No slam on Joey—he's got his own business and seems happy. I just think it's interesting to see where people end up after they give up on the dream. Maybe the only difference between me and him is that I didn't give up, no matter how frustrated and full of doubt I felt at times.

WHEN I FIRST arrived in L.A., I'd sent my head shots to a thousand people, as you know. I re-sent them to hundreds, including to the casting offices at soap operas. When I mailed to *General Hospital*, I put a Post-it note right above my face that said, "Casting: I'm ready to operate." I just couldn't send a picture without a pun. It's like a sickness.

They must have liked my enthusiasm, because a week later, I got called in to be Office Worker #4. The job was to enter the "office" set with a folder and say, "Where do you want me to file this, boss?"

It was my network television debut. My mother told everybody she knew. My father asked, "You get paid?"

"Yeah."

"Up front?"

"Right after."

"In cash?"

They paid $234 for the day (by check), which was the equivalent of two eight-hour shifts at the Four Seasons. That meant I could work one less shift at the lounge and devote the time to comedy instead. Everything related back to comedy and earning enough to do it. Being an extra on soaps seemed like a gold mine. I needed more of that. I let the *GH* extras casting person know that I was available and ready to work. I'd carry a whole box of folders if they needed me to.

I started getting regular spots on *GH*, *Days of Our Lives*, and *Port Charles*, in a wide range of parts with no emotional depth, like Cop #2, Surgeon #1, or Patron #3. Every part came with a number. The only number I cared about was $234.

Being an extra isn't anything close to acting, but there's no shame in being part of the scenery. In the industry, extras prefer being thought of as "atmosphere." I didn't care what they called me. These jobs were cake. I'd show up 9:30 a.m., put on my costume, hang around until two or three, eat for free, get the call to walk across the set, occasionally deliver a single line of dialogue (like "You're under arrest!" or "Scalpel, STAT!"), then clock out and get paid.

In addition to standup and soaps, I auditioned for roles in sitcoms. The first thing I learned was that sitcom auditions were cattle calls. I'd walk into a room and find fifteen or twenty actors, all of us the same age, all of us with more or less the same look, all of us desperate to book a part in a sitcom that usually amounted to one scene with five or six lines tops, if you were lucky. I'd walk into these casting sessions, look around the room at all the other actors, and ask myself, *How the hell are these producers going to tell us apart?* I had to distinguish myself in some way, separate myself from the pack.

I'll use my marketing chops, I thought. They already had my head shot. What could I send them that would make them remember me?

A pizza. I tried it once, and sent a pizza to the casting director named Penny with a note: "Thanks for seeing me. Enjoy your lunch." My friend Mike played the delivery guy. He walked into the room carrying the pie, and said, "Hey, Penny,

I'm out here ten years, delivering pizzas, and this guy comes into the shop just now and orders a pie to go, for you. He wanted you to have it. Open it up. He put the pepperonis into a cent sign for Penny. Unbelievable. We started talking. Funniest guy I ever seen in my life. You seen this guy?"

"Yeah," she said. "We just saw him. Thanks for the tip. We are going in a different direction, but leave the pie."

This did not get me a callback or a part. I really thought someone would offer me a job because of the creative combo of inventiveness and pepperonis. For me, hope springs delusional.

SINCE MY EXTRA work on *GH*, I'd picked up a few parts here and there over the years. A bouncer in a TV show called *Complete Savages*. A low-rent gangster in *Cruise*, a small independent film. I watched comedians I came up with land TV development deals and star in sitcoms. Nothing like that happened for me.

Until 2015! After seventeen years in comedy, I finally got a deal with NBC to write the pilot episode of a sitcom based on my life, called *Sebastian Says*. This deal was years in the making. My team and I cycled through a few writers and showrunners before we locked in with a writer named Austen Earl. Austen and I originally met in 2012 to talk about the possibility of collaborating on a sitcom. We hit it off and wanted to work together, but right after our meeting, he got an exclusive gig and wasn't allowed to develop anywhere else. I was so disappointed. I felt like I'd found and lost my guy.

A few years later, when I was putting the pieces together for *Sebastian Says*, I reached out to Austen again, and was thrilled that he was available. In all the years of meeting writers, I'd never clicked with anyone like I did with him. We had a lot in common. We come from the same type of background: a blue-collar family. He married a woman from an upper-class family. We're both driven, have a sense of humor, and ride scooters. You don't find too many guys who drive Vespas. The only minor difference was he went to Brown, an Ivy League school, and studied American literature, while I went to Northern Illinois, where I reprimanded my fraternity brothers for pissing in Tri Sig's mailbox.

Austen and I used our similarities to pitch to the network. "He's middle class, I'm middle class," I said at meetings. "He married into a wealthy family, I married into one. He drives a Vespa, I drive a Vespa. We see the world the same way. We understand each other's lives." On the strength of that, we were able to convince NBC to give us a deal, and Greg Garcia (*My Name Is Earl*, *The Millers*, and *Yes, Dear*) came on board. Suddenly, I had a network deal and was in business with Greg, a well-respected showrunner. The pieces were lining up.

It didn't take long for Austen and me to hash out the script. I'd give him the characters, and he formulated the dialogue.

He would call me up about this situation or that one and ask, "What would your father say?" "What would Lana say?" The show was all about the tension between my old-school, set-in-his-ways immigrant father and my young wife and her modern California sensibility, with me in the middle. Loosely, my life.

Script in hand, the network gave us the green light to make a pilot episode, so now we had to find actors to play the other parts. The three big roles were me, my wife, and my father. The network gave us a list of every actor in all of Hollywood who could pass for an Italian aged between sixty-five and sixty-eight years old. Robert De Niro, Joe Pesci, and Joe Mantegna were on the list. It was hundreds of names long, anybody who fit the description. I didn't even need the list. I already knew who I wanted to play my father: Tony Danza. I grew up watching Tony and felt as if I were already related to him. People told me growing up that I looked like him, and it made me feel cool. He was a veteran of two long-running hit sitcoms (*Taxi* and *Who's the Boss?*). He hadn't done one since then, so it would be awesome to bring him into ours. I could see the headline: "Tony Danza Plays Up-and-Coming Comedian's Father on New NBC Show *Sebastian Says*."

Greg got the script to Tony, and he responded within twenty-four hours to say he loved it and he was in! He gravitated toward the relationship between the father and the son: "This is how I grew up," he said. "And I have a son. I get it."

It was exactly what I'd hoped to hear. For me, this news was another one of these moments when I couldn't believe a guy I grew up watching and admiring was interested in working with me.

Negotiations with Tony took a while. I had no idea what was going on, and I didn't care. I was just happy to be in the game, working with Austen and Greg and, most likely, Tony Danza. Finally, after a few weeks and a lot of back-and-forth, Tony officially signed on. It was really happening! We had locked in a TV legend. It felt like we couldn't miss.

As soon as the ink was dry on his contract, I reached out to Tony by DMing him on Twitter, writing, "Hey, man, I'm so excited that you're doing the show. What a dream come true. Can't wait to meet you and learn from the best. Here is my personal information."

He called and left a message that I didn't get right away because Lana and I were in Maui, where I had a corporate gig. When we got to our hotel room I saw the voicemail, and I played it for my wife. He said, "Hey, man, it's Tony. I'm really looking forward to this. Give me a call." It was one of those messages that, in the old days, the answering machine would have cut off it was so long. He sounded just like Tony Banta or Tony Micelli, that iconic voice that made listening to a message from him surreal. Lana and I just stared at each other in shock, replaying it, and she said, "Fucking Tony Danza just called you."

For the rest of the trip, we would say "Fucking Tony Danza" out of the blue, look at one another, and laugh.

I called him back and suggested we meet before the upcoming table read of the script. He invited me to Florida to see his Frank Sinatra–type show where he sings with a band and does jokes in between songs, but I explained that I was unable to come because of the Maui gig. We decided to meet in New York for dinner the following week.

I walked into Patsy's, an iconic Italian joint on West 56th Street with photos on the walls of famous people who'd eaten there. Tony was already in the back corner booth, holding court.

The first thing I noticed about Tony Danza: He's got a crooked pinkie finger from boxing. Second thing: He is very nice, very personable. He knew every waiter by name, like, "Hey, Frank. Another martini for my friend." Third thing: He has lived an incredible life and has so many stories that we could've sat there until morning. From Frank Sinatra stories, to his kids, his career, his fantastic cheese shop in Little Italy called Alleva Dairy, I could have listened all night. He's sixty-five but has the energy of a thirty-year-old. I asked him question after question, like "How do sitcoms work? What can I expect?" I didn't know *anything*, but he knew everything, and was only too happy to tell me. He also shared that he'd been researching his part in *Sebastian Says*, and he had assembled a New York City cast of characters who resembled the ones on the show so he could practice. I'd never even heard of someone doing that, and I was blown away that he was doing all this work and really diving in to make the show a hit.

We closed the place down. It felt like I'd known him forever. Tony was so down to earth and present. We ended the night taking a photo with a Frank Sinatra statue in the restaurant like any two good Italian boys should.

The next day, I met the pilot director, Scott Ellis. I talked to him about what to expect, too. I was going into uncharted territory. Part of me was a little worried that I wasn't going to be able to make it work. The show was written by Austen and me, starring me, based on my life, with my name in the title. The pressure was *on*. It was up to me to make the pilot good enough to air. If I established somewhat of a relationship with Tony Danza and the director before we got started on the production, it would be easier to hit the ground running and feel more confident on the set.

I went back to L.A. and worked with Greg on every aspect of the show. The wardrobe, the setting, the casting. Lana was deep into curating all the visuals. When they designed the set, they made a miniature 3D model of it. They asked about every decision, from what fabric should go on the couch to the paintings on the walls. My wife is a perfectionist and always pushes for improvement. If they asked me, "Which color for the curtains?" I'd just pick one, but Lana would say, "Do you have another shade of purple?" In the beginning of our relationship,

I used to get frustrated with her because she was so meticulous. But now I've learned to trust her with all things creative, and when I see how her vision comes to life I'm always like, "Okay, now I get it."

One of the biggest challenges that we had was casting the character of my wife. It took me thirty-five years to find Lana, and here I was trying to find someone to play her in two weeks! After seeing a lot of the actresses, none of them right, Lana said, "I can do it," and started reading the lines with me. She was trying to help and had always secretly wanted to act, but this was not the time to do it. I needed an experienced pro for my pilot.

I sat through every audition, which gave me an entirely different perspective on the audition process. Now that I was on the other side of the table, I understood that you know in an instant if someone is right for the part. As soon as actors filed in, you could see the nerves, the discomfort. People would make forced and awkward small talk. They may have been great actors, but for the most part, they were not able to act relaxed.

From where I sat, I was rooting for every person who came in. The thing actors don't always realize is that the people watching hope you will do well and make their jobs easier. We wanted them to knock it out of the park. When they didn't, it was always a disappointment. Casting is a laborious, long process. There were different opinions in the room, too. I only cared about whether someone was funny enough. I talked to Jerry after this process. "In casting *Seinfeld*," he said, "people had to make me laugh." When you're doing a sitcom, the actors have to have that quality. If they're not making you laugh, they do not belong on the show. The network and other voices involved had other things to consider. In the end, we did put together a great cast, but I believe the overall vision of the show had been touched by too many hands.

After seeing scores of actresses, Vanessa Lachey was the standout for the part of my wife, and really nailed her audition. Lana saw her tape and agreed she was a fantastic choice. We then cast the supporting parts—the sister-in-law, her husband, their kid, my character's friends, and the tiny world of *Sebastian Says* was populated. So we had a script, a cast, a set, wardrobe, a director, a showrunner. It was a week out from taping and we were finally good to go.

Or so I thought. Network had a problem with the script. We did a table read—all the actors reading their lines, but not standing up and acting them—in front of a few executives. After we finished, the network head said there were a few things he didn't like. Like, the entire plot of the script.

The pilot told the story of how my father wanted to murder a possum in the backyard (material straight from my act) by putting antifreeze on bologna, and my wife wanted to do it in a more humane way. The underlings had requested that we use this story for the pilot and told us they thought it was the perfect idea. But the network head didn't like it. Did the underlings then defend the script and tell their boss what they'd been telling us? No. It wouldn't have mattered if they had. Whatever the head guy liked, they had to agree with. Whatever he didn't like, they fell in line with that, too.

Austen and I had to go back to the drawing board. We went with something totally made up, about Tony's character passing his apron, the one he always wore to cook Sunday supper, down to me so I could pick up the tradition. Part of the reason for the Sunday supper idea was to get everyone in the cast on the stage. It wasn't enough to just have the three main characters talking in the yard. The passing-the-baton concept wasn't from my real life and it felt contrived. But we worked with the parameters we were given, and in the end, I loved the script. The relationships between the characters were well established. I couldn't have been more confident in Austen. He is a wordsmith and his comedic chops are outstanding. One of the jokes was about my having a problem with my wife's half sister coming to Sunday supper.

She said, "She's my sister."

I said, "She's your *half* sister. So we don't *have* to invite her to everything." A little play on words there. Austen gave me great material to work with, and I believed the pilot was good enough for the network to order six or seven more episodes. We'd have a chance to breathe a bit and take it further.

Finally, after six months plus of hard work to get to this point, we were ready to shoot the pilot of *Sebastian Says* at CBS

Bradford Studios, on the same stage where *Seinfeld* had been filmed for nine years. The vibes couldn't have been better.

It was a big night, a big deal. My in-laws were in town. My mother, father, and sister were coming. Everyone was going to be there for the taping. The shoot would be the first time we performed it in front of a live audience. As a comedian, I was excited to hear the real laughter. During the dress rehearsals, the studio had been empty except for the cast and crew. If you tell a joke in a studio where no one can hear it, is it still funny? At the taping, we'd find out.

Basically, I was shitting. Totally nervous. I'd never done anything like this before. We started the opening scene, with Vanessa and me in a Whole Foods and how the store bothered me. There was a guy giving a massage, another touting the many uses of argan oil. A shopper (Shopper #5) wore hemp clothing, and I commented that it only comes in two colors— oatmeal and throw-up. Then when we checked out at the cashier, it came out that I'd forgotten the reusable bags at home. I told the guy to just throw our stuff in the paper bag, and he judged me for not bringing my bag made of wheat. In the next scene, I walked in the door to our home with all the groceries piled in my sweater and I dumped them on the table.

It was a funny bit, and we were getting laughs. But the director would yell, "Cut," and suggest we reshoot the scene. The idea was to get the best take possible, but when we repeated the scene—or a single line—over and over, the audience knew the joke was coming. In my act, I'd never stop after a bit and say, "Hold on, guys. I didn't do that quite right. I'm going to do it again."

The jerky pace of the shoot took some getting used to. Sometimes, Austen and Greg would come out of the bullpen (where they were watching the camera playback) and give me line changes and gesture modifications, one after the other, like, "Change *this*, and say *that*, and move *here*, and not *there*." I'd been terrified of forgetting my lines and had memorized everything painstakingly. And now they wanted me to change it?

I listened and nodded, but I was thinking, *Oh, fuck*. I couldn't remember ten notes about two lines of dialogue on the fly. Meanwhile, the audience sat up there, waiting for action. It was way more nerve-wracking than doing standup. In my act, I know what I'm going to say. I'm in control of it. But I wasn't in control when I was being told what to do, how to say a word, stand, cross the stage, turn left (FYI: you can't turn your back on the audience, ever). The nuances of shooting a sitcom were infinite, and I had to learn them *while we were filming*.

With all that going on, it was impossible for me to judge how the shoot went. I thought we'd done a great job. After we finished, my father came down to the set, full of compliments. He started talking to Tony, offering to help him with his research. Lana and Vanessa were like kindred spirits. My sister and Mom took pictures with Tony and the cast, and were obviously excited to be there. Seeing my family happy about my big night brought me out of my worry and into the moment. It meant a lot to have all of them there—my parents, wife, in-laws, sister, brother-in-law. I don't love a crowd outside of standup, but this was nice. I felt like everybody was on this journey with me, that we were on the ride together. That feeling of joy will get even more intense when Serafina is older and I can bring her to a sitcom taping.

Not *Sebastian Says*, unfortunately.

Serafina might see the pilot episode one day. No one else ever will.

A lot goes into the decision about which pilots the network will pick up for each TV season. They look at what's currently on the air, what's doing well, and what makes sense to follow a hit TV show. I don't know every factor they considered or how they made their final cut, but in the end, they did not pick up my show. We were completely shocked and heartbroken. That year, NBC made ten pilots and took three.

The odds were against us from the beginning, and I knew that. But I believed we'd get through. When we didn't, it was crushing. You put your blood, sweat, and tears, your whole life story, into this one thing, and then, in an instant, it's done.

I could just go back on the road, back to comedy. For me, the TV show would actually have been a pay cut compared to what I made touring. (But it wasn't about the money, of course.) I felt terrible for the actors. We'd been gearing up for what would be years of an on-stage family. They were banking on the network ordering twelve episodes so they'd have steady work. Now the actors would have to psych themselves up to go through that audition process again, and keep hitting it until they landed on a show with a future.

How much of the show's failure was my fault? I tortured myself with this question in the months to follow. Did I, we, do our best? Did we give all we could? Looking back, I think we did, but you always want to go above and beyond. Lana came to the emotional rescue, and said, "The sitcom not working out clears the way for something else that will." Only time would tell if she was right.

THE SITCOM'S DEATH wasn't it for me as an actor. I finally got my big break playing the pivotal role as Johnny the Groundhog in *The Nut Job 2: Nutty by Nature*. By the time you read this, I'm sure I'll have received my Oscar. (I brought my six-year-old niece to the red carpet premiere, and she was in heaven.)

I still wanted to see my face on screen, not just my voice coming through a rodent's mouth, so I took what is known in Hollywood as "general meetings." You go in, sit down with producers and directors just to talk and see if they have any projects that might be right for you, now and in the future. It's like, "Nice to meet you. Keep me in mind." Early in my career, I would have gone home from one of these meetings and waited with bated breath for the phone to ring and a producer to tell me he was going to cast me in a movie. But having been in the business for a while, and gone up and down the emotional roller coaster, I knew not to get my hopes up, especially having created the pilot and seen the politics of actually getting a role or a show on the air. I learned firsthand how these things are so out of my control. So now I'd walk out of general meetings and go on to the next thing without putting any pressure or expectations on anything. If the stars lined up and we both found that working together was a good creative fit, then it would pan out. I would leave the meeting and say, "If the phone rings, it rings, great. If it doesn't, at least I have my comedy career to fall back on." I always feel for actors because, for most of them, that is not the case.

I was so comfortable with *not* getting acting roles that when I did get a call about appearing in a movie called *Tag* with Ed Helms, John Hamm, and Jeremy Renner, I wasn't all that excited about it. I would play a small part as a minister in a wedding scene, with a few lines and, according to my agent, "some improv." I don't like to improv in front of a camera. It's hard enough to memorize the lines and come in on cue, but now I'd have to wing it? My agent convinced me to do it, saying it would be a good opportunity to be on camera in a big comedy. I couldn't deny that and agreed to do it.

In hindsight, maybe I wasn't so excited about it because I was scared of doing something new. I'd never acted in a big movie before. Could I pull it off? Could I hold my own, doing an improv scene with Ed Helms? Jeremy Renner had been nominated for an Oscar, *twice*. I'd been Surgeon #1 on *General Hospital*.

Along with fears about remembering my lines, I was anxious about how it all worked. My first day, I walked onto the Atlanta set of a movie that had been in production already for three weeks. I was the new guy. I didn't know anyone. They'd already established their cliques. It was first-day-at-a-new-school-type shit. I had a tight group of friends in junior high, but when we had to move up, all of them went to one high school and I was alone at another one. It had to do with your address. They were all zoned for a different school even though we lived near each other. My first day, I didn't know anyone and was really shy. In the cafeteria, I ate alone. I watched all the other kids talking and laughing, while I sat there, miserable, believing that it would be like that every day for the next four years. Of course, it didn't work out that way. But the dread was so gut-wrenching, I never forgot it. Whenever I feel acutely awkward and alone, I get a flashback, which happened on my first day on the set of *Tag*.

The scene was in a large park, outside, and they had me in a black suit. I was gushing three different types of sweat: (1) regular sweat that is my everyday norm (I run hot), (2) sweat from wearing a black wool suit in Atlanta in 100 degree heat, and (3) a cold, damp nervous sweat. I was losing so much water, my mouth went dry, and I was smacking my lips to get any moisture in there while going over my lines. I went wet and dry. I didn't know anyone. I'd never done this before.

Then a knock on the door, and it was a production assistant who said, "They're ready for you on set."

My heart started beating like crazy, and I thought, *This is new.* My heart didn't beat like this when I went in front of eighteen thousand people to do standup. But to film a scene in front of a few people? You would have been able to visually see my heart beating if I removed my shirt. So I followed the PA to the set, and it wasn't the quaint small scene I'd imagined. There were a hundred extras, plus a whole wedding party. As the minister/pastor/whatever, I was going to officiate the ceremony.

Much to my great relief, I saw a familiar face. It was the producer whom I'd had a general meeting with. As he walked over to me, I thought, *Oh cool, I'll be able to hang by him and shoot the shit. Here we go. No more awkward feelings as if I don't know anyone. We can have lunch together,* etc. etc. Next thing I know, he said, "I know you from somewhere," like we hadn't sat across a table from each other for an hour a few months ago. This played on my mind, too. It wasn't a "Don't you know who I am?" ego moment. It was an anxious "Does anyone know why I'm here?" moment.

Nearby, I saw Renner, Helms, and Hamm talking to each other. The old me would have gone in a corner and waited for someone to drag me out. But I made myself visible to them by walking over and introducing myself. It was low-key, like,

"Hey, I'm Sebastian. What's going on?" Pleasantries were exchanged, and then they went back to what they'd been talking about before I went over. *So now what?* I thought. Should I chime in? Pretend I see someone else that I needed to talk to? Make a joke and then peel away? While the three of them talked, I stood there planning my escape route. Usually, in this sort of situation, I try to leave on a laugh. Wait for people to crack up and then do a laughing 180-degree-turn peel-off exit. I was so in my head because I wanted to talk to these guys, but I also needed to run my lines. I didn't want to be the forty-four-year-old guy who fucked up the scene because he was too busy trying to find someone to play with at recess.

A few minutes later, I was called onto the set and I met Leslie Bibb, the female lead. She took one look at me and said, "Size two boots! You do a Prince bit, right? I love that! You're so funny!"

I thought, *Thank God.* Someone was familiar with my comedy. It was a moment of validation, one I really needed to feel more at ease on this movie. Sometimes, you need a little external support to give you a boost of confidence, that's all. Standing in our places, I talked a little bit to Renner. I was feeling more comfortable and ready to deliver my lines.

Then the director adjusted the lines and added backstory that threw a wrench into my whole plan! He told me to just do what I do, basically saying, "Don't worry about sticking to the lines."

I said, "Okay, no problem!"—but in my head, I was going, *Fuck!* But I just did it anyway. I learned that sometimes, when the pressure is on and you're pushed into a situation that's unexpected, it's more natural and organic.

On stage, I can hear people laughing, and that lets me know that what is coming out of my mouth is funny and things are going well. But on a movie set, you do your lines, and it's completely quiet. I didn't hear anything. The whole time, I was making up lines, having to rely on my internal comedic radar and to trust that what I was saying was funny. All you can do is prepare for what you know, trust in yourself, and that things will iron themselves out. (FYI: I just got a peek at the edited scene last week. It turned out fantastic!)

With each take, my confidence grew, and I walked away from the set of *Tag* determined to do more acting. This experience was the first time I really had the opportunity to sink my teeth into a part and adapt my comedic skills to a new and unfamiliar art form. I'm so glad I did it, and I proved to myself that I could hold my own with some really great actors. Having a comedic movie role, where I had some creative freedom, was a huge step. Now that I have that under my belt, I'm excited for the phone to ring with more opportunities. Now that I know I can do it, I have the confidence to pull it off.

LAST BITE

When I do interviews, people always ask, "What's next for you?"

I have absolutely no idea.

It's best if you don't know.

Yes, it's great to have goals in life and make plans, to have ambitions and big picture ideas. But, looking back, I see that every break I got came totally out of the blue. I was working hard every day to advance my career, but what actually pushed me forward were those chance encounters—like being in the Comedy Store parking lot with Dice or in the stairway at Dublin's with Vince. The things I plotted—like my sitcom, literally—didn't turn out like I'd hoped. And other things panned out in unpredictable ways. For instance, if I hadn't done the film *Cruise*, I wouldn't have had tape of my dramatic acting to show to casting directors to get work in the movies.

Fitting the filming of *Cruise* into my schedule was nearly

impossible. I flew back and forth from New York to Florida four times in one week to make it happen. I was totally stressed out, but something in my gut told me to make it work. At the time, I didn't know if it was going to be worth it. And now I've learned that my scene in it pushed me over the edge to land a part in a movie coming out next year.

Some people might have ready answers to "What's next?" off the top of their heads. They have a running list of everything they want to do, like opening a cheese shop in Manhattan, having five kids, winning an Oscar, or earning seven figures. My philosophy is that if you plan too much, you might miss the random, unforeseen opportunities that could turn you around but ultimately take you where you want to go.

Whatever happens is what happens. What's next is what's next. How's that for a life philosophy? Five years ago, I couldn't have predicted where I'd end up; I can't predict where I'll be five years from now.

My only plan has always been to make people laugh. I set out to be a standup comedian, that's it. I never thought that I'd be sitting where I am now, writing this book in Los Angeles with my amazing wife in our beautiful home with our adorable baby sleeping with her arms above her head like a starfish upstairs. The days of gazing out the window at a lunatic humping his couch are long gone. I never imagined that my career in standup comedy would go as well as it has, or that I would find true love. And when I say true love, I mean a girl who monitors my caloric intake, makes me literally run up mountains, and found a nail lady to come to the house who also drops crab apples and passion fruit from her garden in our mailbox on a random Tuesday. I could never have ever planned these things or made this shit up. I just stayed hungry and worked for everything that came my way. It's all I could do, and what I plan on doing in the future.

In this business, there's a fine line between reality and negativity. The iron is hot for me now, but it could burn out. Disappointment could be around the corner. I don't know. And that's the whole point: *No one knows anything.*

Apologies to my wife, who likes to think everything is good and will keep on being that way. I'm more comfortable believing that I could fall off the mountain at any time. Maybe that's what fuels me to dig in to hang on. I look at guys like the Rock or Kevin Hart, who are always positive, with an attitude like "I'm at the top of the mountain, but I'm going farther. I'm going to the moon!" Looking up at the moon might work for them. But what motivates and fuels me is looking down at my feet, and putting one in front of the other.

ACKNOWLEDGMENTS

Believe me when I tell you I had a lot of help putting this book in your hands.

In anything I do in my career, my wife, Lana, is right by my side. I couldn't have done this book without her. She really knew how to translate my stories to the page. It was a long and laborious process, but we did it, babe.

Val Frankel, my cowriter, for getting my voice and breaking her ass to make this book what it is. When I met her in Atlantic City and we worked over the weekend, I knew I was in good hands. Thanks for giving me the confidence to make this book a hit.

My manager, Judi Marmel, the hardest-working woman in show business, for pushing me to places I never thought possible. Who knew we'd go from lunch at the Islands Cafe to a bestselling book?

ACKNOWLEDGMENTS

My agent, Anthony Mattero, for being patient with me and allowing me to make this book what I knew it could be.

The entire team at Simon & Schuster for taking a chance on a first-time writer and giving me an opportunity to tell my story: Jeremie Ruby-Strauss, Brita Lundberg, Jennifer Bergstrom, and Jennifer Robinson.

My PR team, Ebie McFarland, Debbie Keller, and Nicole Greene, for getting the word to the people that I have a book. Thanks for your tireless dedication and getting me quality press.

My agents at UTA, my lawyer Greg Gellman, and my business managers, Leo Jenkins and John Power.

Chris and Steve Mazzilli for long talks over a Milo's special.

Thanks to my mom, dad, and sister, Jessica, and the Dadon family for always believing in me and never letting me quit.

Alex Goodman and Rachel Williams and everyone at LEG for your hard work. It doesn't go unnoticed.

Thanks to Georgina Morrison for being eight steps ahead of me and for her passion and commitment to all things Maniscalco.

Thanks to the Lutgert family for always supporting me.

To all my fans, who have supported me since day one. Thanks for spreading the word about my comedy and showing up to my shows and now buying my book.

And to my daughter, Serafina, who is not old enough to read this yet, but when you do I want you to know you are my little angel and you make every day more exciting than the last.